GENESIS to REVELATION

A Comprehensive Verse-by-Verse Exploration of the Bible

LUKE
HORACE R. WEAVER

LEADER GUIDE

GENESIS to REVELATION

A Comprehensive Verse-by-Verse Exploration of the Bible

LUKE
HORACE R. WEAVER

LEADER GUIDE

GENESIS TO REVELATION SERIES: **LUKE**
LEADER GUIDE

ABINGDON PRESS
Nashville
Copyright © 1984, 1985, 1987 by Graded Press.
Revised Edition Copyright © 1997 by Abingdon Press.
Updated and Revised Edition Copyright © 2018 by Abingdon Press
All rights reserved.

ISBN 9781501855092

Manufactured in the United States of America
18 19 20 21 22 23 24 25 26 27—10 9 8 7 6 5 4 3 2 1

HOW TO TEACH GENESIS TO REVELATION

Unique Features of This Bible Study

In Genesis to Revelation, you and your class will study the Bible in three steps. Each step provides a different level of understanding of the Scripture. We call these steps Dimension One, Dimension Two, and Dimension Three.

Dimension One concerns what the Bible actually says. You do not interpret the Scripture at this point; you merely take account of what it says. Your main goal for this dimension is to get the content of the passage clear in your mind. What does the Bible say?

Dimension One is in workbook form. The members of the class will write the answers to questions about the passage in the space provided in the participant book. All the questions in Dimension One can be answered by reading the Bible itself. Be sure the class finishes Dimension One before going on to Dimensions Two and Three.

Dimension Two concerns information that will shed light on the Scripture under consideration. Dimension Two will answer such questions as

- What are the original meanings of some of the words used in the passage?

- What is the original background of the passage?

- Why was the passage most likely written?

- What are the relationships between the persons mentioned in the passage?

- What geographical and cultural factors affect the meaning of the passage?

The question for Dimension Two is, What information do we need in order to understand the meaning of the passage? In Dimension One the class members will discover what the Bible says. In Dimension Two they will discover what the Bible means.

Dimension Three focuses on interpreting the Scripture and applying it to life situations. The questions here are

- What is the meaning of the passage for my life?

- What response does the passage require of me as a Christian?

- What response does this passage require of us as a group?

Dimension Three questions have no easy answers. The task of applying the Scripture to life situations is up to you and the class.

Aside from the three-dimensional approach, another unique feature of this study is the organization of the series as a whole. Classes that choose to study the Genesis to Revelation Series will be able to study all the books of the Bible in their biblical order. This method will give the class continuity that is not present in most other Bible studies. The class will read and study virtually every verse of the Bible, from Genesis straight through to Revelation.

Weekly Preparation

Begin planning for each session early in the week. Read the passage that the lesson covers, and write the answers to Dimension One questions in the participant book. Then read Dimensions Two and Three in the participant book. Make a note of any questions or comments you have. Finally, study the material in the leader guide carefully. Decide how you want to organize your class session.

Organizing the Class Session

Since Genesis to Revelation involves three steps in studying the Scripture, you will want to organize your class sessions around these three dimensions. Each lesson in the participant book and this leader guide consists of three parts.

The first part of each lesson in the leader guide is the same as the Dimension One section in the participant book, except that the leader guide includes the answers to Dimension One questions. These questions and answers are taken from the New International Version of the Bible.

You might use Dimension One in several ways:

1. Ask the group members to read the Scripture and to write the answers to all the Dimension One questions before coming to class. This method will require that the class covenant to spend the necessary amount of study time outside of class. When the class session begins, read through the Dimension One questions, asking for responses from the group members. If anyone needs help with any of the answers, look at the biblical reference together.

2. Or, if you have enough class time, you might spend the first part of the session working through the Dimension One questions together as a group. Locate the Scripture references, ask the questions one at a time, and invite the class members to find the answers and to read them aloud. Then allow enough time for them to write the answers in the participant book.

3. Or, take some time at the beginning of the class session for group members to work individually. Have them read the Dimension One questions and the Scripture references and then write their answers to the questions in the spaces provided in the participant book. Discuss together any questions or answers in Dimension One that do not seem clear. This approach may take longer than the others, but it provides a good change of pace from time to time.

You do not have to organize your class sessions the same way every week. Ask the class members what they prefer. Experiment! You may find ways to study the Dimension One material other than the ones listed above.

The second part of each lesson in this leader guide corresponds to the second part of the participant book lessons. The Dimension Two section of the participant book provides background information to help the participants understand the Scripture. Become familiar with the information in the participant book.

Dimension Two of this leader guide contains additional information on the passage. The leader guide goes into more depth with some parts of the passage than the participant book does. You will want to share this information with the group in whatever way seems appropriate. For example, if someone raises a question about a particular verse, share any additional background information from the leader guide.

You might raise a simple question such as, What words or phrases gave you trouble in understanding the passage? or, Having grasped the content of the passage, what questions remain in your mind? Encourage the group members to share confusing points, troublesome words or phrases, or lingering questions. Write these problems on a posterboard or markerboard. This list of concerns will form the outline for the second portion of the session.

These concerns may also stimulate some research on the part of the group members. If your study group is large enough, divide the class into three groups. Then divide the passage for the following week into three parts. Assign a portion of the passage to each group. Using Bible commentaries and Bible dictionaries, direct each group to discover as much as it can about this portion of the passage before the class meets again. Each group will then report its findings during the class session.

The third part of each lesson in this leader guide relates to Dimension Three in the participant book. This section helps class members discover how to apply the Scripture to their own lives. Here you will find one or more interpretations of the passage—whether traditional, historical, or contemporary. Use these interpretations when appropriate to illumine the passage for the group members.

Dimension Three in the participant book points out some of the issues in the passage that are relevant to our lives. For each of these issues, the participant book raises questions to help the participants assess the meaning of the Scripture for their lives. The information in Dimension Three of the leader guide is designed to help you lead the class in discussing these issues. Usually, you will find a more in-depth discussion of portions of the Scripture.

The discussion in the leader guide will give you a better perspective on the Scripture and its interpretation before you begin to assess its meaning for today. You will probably want to share this Dimension Three information with the class to open the discussion. For each life situation, the leader guide contains suggestions on facilitating the class discussion. You, as the leader, are responsible for group discussions of Dimension Three issues.

Assembling Your Materials

You will need at least three items to prepare for and conduct each class session:

- A leader guide

- A participant book

- A Bible—you may use any translation or several; the answers in this leader guide are taken from the New International Version.

One advantage of the Genesis to Revelation Series is that the study is self-contained. That is, all you need to lead this Bible study is provided for you in the participant books and leader guides. Occasionally, or perhaps on a regular basis, you might want to consult other sources for additional information.

HOW TO LEAD A DISCUSSION

The Teacher as Discussion Leader

As the leader of this series or a part of this series, one of your main responsibilities during each class period will be to lead the class discussion. Some leaders are apprehensive about leading a discussion. In many ways, it is easier to lecture to the class. But remember that the class members will surely benefit more from the class sessions when they actively participate in a discussion of the material.

Leading a discussion is a skill that any teacher can master with practice. And keep in mind—especially if your class is not used to discussion—that the members of your group will also be learning through practice. The following are some pointers on how to lead interesting and thought-provoking discussions in the study group.

Preparing for a Discussion—Where Do I Start?

1. Focus on the subject that will be discussed and on the goal you want to achieve through that discussion.

2. Prepare by collecting information and data that you will need; jot down these ideas, facts, and questions so that you will have them when you need them.

3. Begin organizing your ideas; stop often to review your work. Keep in mind the climate within the group—attitudes, feelings, eagerness to participate and learn.

4. Consider possible alternative group procedures. Be prepared for the unexpected.

5. Having reached your goal, think through several ways to bring the discussion to a close.

As the leader, do not feel that your responsibility is to give a full account or report of the assigned material. This practice promotes dependency. Instead, through stimulating questions and discussion, the participants will read the material—not because you tell them to but because they want to read and prepare.

How Do I Establish a Climate for Learning?

The leader's readiness and preparation quickly establish a climate in which the group can proceed and its members learn and grow. The anxiety and fear of an unprepared leader are contagious but so are the positive vibrations coming from a leader who is prepared to move into a learning enterprise.

An attitude of shared ownership is also basic. Group members need to perceive themselves as part of the learning experience. Persons establish ownership by working on goals, sharing concerns, and accepting major responsibility for learning.

Here are several ways the leader can foster a positive climate for learning and growth.

1. Readiness. A leader who is always fully prepared can promote, in turn, the group's readiness to learn.

2. Exploration. When the leader encourages group members to freely explore new ideas, persons will know they are in a group whose primary function is learning.

3. Exposure. A leader who is open, honest, and willing to reveal himself or herself to the group will encourage participants to discuss their feelings and opinions.

4. Confidentiality. A leader can create a climate for learning when he or she respects the confidentiality of group members and encourages the group members to respect one another's confidentiality.

5. Acceptance. When a leader shows a high degree of acceptance, participants can likewise accept one another honestly.

How Can I Deal With Conflict?

What if conflict or strong disagreement arises in your group? What do you do? Think about the effective and ineffective ways you have dealt with conflict in the past.

Group conflict may come from one of several sources. One common source of conflict involves personality clashes. Any group is almost certain to contain at least two persons whose personalities clash. If you break your class into smaller groups for discussion, be sure these persons are in separate groups.

Another common source of group conflict is subject matter. The Bible can be a very controversial subject. Remember the difference between discussion or disagreement and conflict. As a leader you will have to decide when to encourage discussion and when to discourage conflict that is destructive to the group process.

Group conflict may also come from a general atmosphere conducive to expression of ideas and opinions. Try to discourage persons in the group from being judgmental toward others and their ideas. Keep reminding the class that each person is entitled to his or her own opinions and that no one opinion is more valid than another.

How Much Should I Contribute to the Discussion?

Many leaders are unsure about how much they should contribute to the class discussions. Below are several pitfalls to avoid.

1. The leader should remain neutral on a question until the group has had adequate time to discuss it. At the proper time in the discussion the leader can offer his or her opinion. The leader can direct the questions to the group at large, rechanneling those questions that come to him or her.

    At times when the members need to grapple with a question or issue, the most untimely response a leader can make is answering the question. Do not fall into the trap of doing the group members' work for them. Let them struggle with the question.

    However, if the leader has asked the group members to reveal thoughts and feelings, then group members have the right to expect the same of the leader. A leader has no right to ask others to reveal something he or she is unwilling to reveal. A leader can reveal thoughts and feelings, but at the appropriate time.

    The refusal to respond immediately to a question often takes self-discipline. The leader has spent time thinking, reading, and preparing. Thus the leader usually does have a point of view, and waiting for others to respond calls for restraint.

2. Another pitfall is the leader's making a speech or extended comments in expressing an opinion or summarizing what has been said. For example, in an attempt to persuade others, a leader may speak, repeat, or strongly emphasize what someone says concerning a question.

3. Finally, the pitfall of believing the leader must know "the answers" to the questions is always apparent. The leader need not know all the answers. Many questions that should be raised are ultimate and unanswerable; other questions are open-ended; and still others have several answers.

GENESIS TO REVELATION SERIES
LUKE Leader Guide

Table of Contents

1. Preface, Jesus' Birth, and Boyhood (Luke 1–2)… 12

2. The Key to Jesus' Public Ministry (Luke 3:1–4:30)… 21

3. Jesus' Galilean Ministry (Luke 4:31–6:49)… 31

4. Jesus: Messianic Teacher and Healer (Luke 7–8)… 40

5. The Disciples Accept Jesus as Messiah (Luke 9:1-50)… 50

6. Jesus Sets His Face Toward Jerusalem (Luke 9:51–11:28)… 60

7. True Discipleship and Its Opponents (Luke 11:29–13:9)… 69

8. The Life of Discipleship (Luke 13:10–15:32)… 79

9. The Use and Abuse of Wealth (Luke 16–17)… 89

10. The Kingdom of God (Luke 18:1–19:44)… 97

11. Jesus Responds to Difficult Questions (Luke 19:45–21:38)… 106

12. Jesus Faces His Disciples and Accusers (Luke 22:1–23:25)… 116

13. Jesus Experiences Calvary and Resurrection (Luke 23:26–24:53)… 125

About the Writer

Horace R. Weaver was an editor of the former Department of Adult Publications, The United Methodist Publishing House, who died in 1997. He wrote over one thousand articles and study materials and multiple books.

You will conceive and give birth to a son, and you are to call him Jesus (1:31).

1

PREFACE, JESUS' BIRTH, AND BOYHOOD

Luke 1–2

DIMENSION ONE:
WHAT DOES THE BIBLE SAY?

Answer these questions by reading Luke 1

1. Who is the writer who refers to himself as "I"? (1:3)

The writer never reveals his name. Traditionally, the writer of this Gospel has been identified as Luke, a Gentile physician and traveling companion of Paul (Colossians 4:14).

2. What is the purpose of Luke's Gospel? (1:4)

The purpose of Luke's Gospel is "that you may know the certainty of the things you have been taught."

3. What does Luke say is his method of writing? (1:1-3)

Since many others have written narratives of the events of Jesus' life, "I too decided to write an orderly account."

4. What sources does Luke use in compiling his Gospel? (1:1-2)

Luke's sources are "those who from the first were eyewitnesses and servants of the word."

5. How does Luke describe Herod, Zechariah, and Elizabeth? (1:5-7)

Luke describes Herod as king of Judea, Zechariah as a priest, and his wife Elizabeth as a descendant of Aaron. Zechariah and Elizabeth "were righteous in the sight of God. . . . Elizabeth was not able to conceive, and they were both very old."

6. What is Zechariah doing in the temple? (1:8)

He is "serving as priest before God" when his division is on duty.

7. How does Zechariah respond to the angel's promise of a prophetic son? (1:18, 22)

Zechariah is skeptical of the promise, for "I am an old man and my wife is well along in years." When he comes out of the temple, he cannot speak.

8. What words does Gabriel use to greet Mary? (1:28)

"Greetings, you who are highly favored! The Lord is with you!"

9. Over what people does Gabriel say Jesus will reign? (1:32-33)

God will give him the throne of his father David, and "he will reign over Jacob's descendants forever."

10. What unique, divine event does Gabriel tell Mary will happen in her life? (1:35)

"The Holy Spirit will come on you, and the power of the Most High will overshadow you. So the holy one to be born will be called the Son of God."

11. What does Mary learn about her relative Elizabeth? (1:36)

The angel tells Mary, "Even Elizabeth your relative is going to have a child in her old age."

12. What names does the angel tell Zechariah and Mary to give their sons? (1:13, 31)

The angel tells Zechariah to name his son John and Mary to name her son Jesus.

13. In response to Elizabeth's warm greetings, how does Mary answer? (1:46-47)
    Mary says, "My soul glorifies the Lord / and my spirit rejoices in God my Savior."

14. After staying three months with Elizabeth, where does Mary go? (1:56)
    Mary returns home.

15. How does Zechariah confirm the naming of his son? (1:63)
    Zechariah, still unable to speak, writes on a tablet, "His name is John."

16. One of Luke's special interests is the Holy Spirit. What does he say about the Holy Spirit and Mary, Elizabeth, and Zechariah? (1:35, 41, 67)
    Luke says that the Holy Spirit will come upon Mary, Elizabeth is filled with the Holy Spirit, and Zechariah is filled with the Holy Spirit and prophesies.

17. About whom does Zechariah sing his praises? (1:68-79)
    Zechariah blesses God, the child John, and Jesus.

Answer these questions by reading Luke 2

18. Why are Joseph and Mary going to Bethlehem? (2:1-5)
    Caesar Augustus has ordered a census of the people, with each head of the house returning to his ancestral home. Since Joseph is of the house and lineage of David, he and Mary are going to Bethlehem, David's town.

19. What is the message of the heavenly host to the shepherds? (2:14)
    "Glory to God in the highest heaven, / and on earth peace to those on whom his favor rests."

20. What happens on the eighth day after Jesus' birth? (2:21)
    At the end of eight days, the baby Jesus is circumcised and given his name.

21. What do Mary and Joseph offer as a sacrifice to make atonement for Mary? (2:22-24)
    They offer, according to Jewish law, "a pair of doves or two young pigeons."

22. What do Joseph and Mary do after meeting the requirements of the law? (2:39)
    They return "to their own town of Nazareth."

23. How often do Joseph and Mary visit Jerusalem? (2:41)
    Joseph and Mary visit Jerusalem every year for the Festival of the Passover.

24. When Jesus is twelve, what is he doing at the temple, after the Festival of the Passover? (2:42-49)
    His parents find him "in the temple courts, sitting among the teachers, listening to them and asking them questions."

25. How does Luke describe Jesus' growth and development? (2:52)
    "Jesus grew in wisdom and stature, and in favor with God and man."

DIMENSION TWO:
WHAT DOES THE BIBLE MEAN?

The Gospel of Luke and the Acts of the Apostles make up one-fourth of the New Testament. These two books represent slightly fewer verses than all the thirteen letters of Paul plus the Letter to the Hebrews. But Luke and Acts represent much more than sheer bulk in the New Testament. They bring much that is new, such as Luke 9:51–18:14. They also show the compiler's (Luke's) use of many sources of information, such as Mark's Gospel (which became the basic outline for the Gospels of Luke and Matthew); the writings that only the Gospels of Luke and Matthew hold in common (known by scholars as *Q*); and the special and unique source that only Luke has (designated by scholars as the *L* source). A comparison of the Gospel of Luke with the Gospel of Mark shows how the writer felt free to correct, change, and grammatically improve sections used in Mark. In similar reports, Luke smooths out Mark's involved sentence structure:

Mark 3:7-8. "Jesus withdrew with his disciples to the lake, and a large crowd from Galilee followed. When they heard about all he was doing, many people came to him from Judea, Jerusalem, Idumea, and the regions across the Jordan and around Tyre and Sidon."

Luke 6:17-18a. "A large crowd of his disciples was there and a great number of people from all over Judea, from Jerusalem, and from the coastal region around Tyre and Sidon, who had come to hear him."

As is true of the other Gospel writers, Luke wrote in Greek and clearly used the Septuagint (Greek) translation of the Old Testament. He was a fine Greek scholar who knew his language well. Some of Luke's poems and descriptions are unexcelled in verbal beauty. (See 1:46-55, 68-79.)

The Scripture in this session is divided into six themes:

1. Preface: Writer's Purpose in Writing (1:1-4)
2. The Promise to Zechariah of the Birth of John (1:5-25)
3. The Promise to Mary of the Birth of Jesus (1:26-38) and Her Visit to Elizabeth (1:39-56)
4. The Birth of John (1:57-80)
5. The Birth of Jesus (2:1-20)
6. Jesus' Infancy and Childhood (2:21-52)

Luke 1:1-4. In no place throughout the Gospel of Luke does the writer identify himself. In Acts 1:1 the writer states, "In my former book, Theophilus, I wrote about all that Jesus began to do and to teach." In Luke 1:3, we read, "I too decided to write." The early church fathers identified the *I* of Acts and the *I* of the Gospel with Luke the physician. If so, he is the physician named in Colossians 4:14.

In the Gospel and in Acts, Luke is writing to a person named Theophilus. The word *Theophilus* means "loved of God," so some have assumed that Luke wrote to anyone who loves God. But Luke seems to be writing to a friend, possibly a Roman or Greek benefactor, who is a person of considerable prestige—hence Luke's phrase "most excellent Theophilus."

Whoever it is, Luke writes for him "an orderly account." The purpose of the Gospel is "that you may know the certainty of the things you have been taught."

Luke's description of his method of writing the Gospel is valuable to us. He describes his method as one of research for information from as many sources as he could find—all around Palestine, the Near East (as in Ephesus, Antioch, Troas), and Europe (as in Athens, Corinth, Berea). Luke would have known of, heard, and observed the lifestyles and faith claims of Christians such as Peter, James, Lydia, Priscilla, Timothy, and Mary. Luke heard hundreds of witnesses to the person and teachings of Jesus while Luke worshiped at Corinth, Athens, Antioch, Caesarea, Ephesus, Philippi, Jerusalem, and Rome. Luke prayed with them. He witnessed with them. He knew how they interpreted the Old Testament in terms of the life and teachings of Jesus. Luke experienced the Holy Spirit at work in each of these churches. Yes, and he must have taken many notes for later use in his two volumes about Jesus and the disciples.

From scores of notes, written documents (such as the teachings of Jesus [an undiscovered document identified by scholars as *Q*] and the Gospel of Mark), and his memories of many witnesses and ministers of the word, the writer compiled his orderly account that we know as the Gospel of Luke.

Point out to participants that the authenticity of the Gospel of Luke depends on the authenticity of Luke's sources—of witnesses; of ministers of the word; and of persons he talked to, such as Peter, James, Mary, and many others. These kinds of questions are pertinent to our sincere quest for what the Bible means. Interpretation, exegesis (scholarly investigation), and commentary depend on the value given each source. To put it another way, Is every passage in the Bible—and in Luke—equally valid? Or were some sources more valid than others? Would the social, political, and religious conditions of AD 50 cause Christian interpreters to change or omit some of Jesus' sayings? For example, in Mark's Gospel, Jesus notes that the temple is a house of prayer for people of all nations (Mark 11:17). But Luke omits the reference to people of all nations worshiping in the temple. (See Luke 19:46.) Might Luke (who wrote in AD 80–85) have omitted such a reference because the temple no longer existed, having been destroyed by the Romans in AD 70? Luke was a careful thinker, free of contradictions.

Luke 1:5-25. The author includes dates, rulers, and names of persons. In 1:5, Luke tells us that Herod was king of Judea. Theophilus would have known that Herod ruled Judea from 37 BC–4 BC and that the end of his reign (4 BC) was marked by the birth of two male infants, John and Jesus ("so that you may know the certainty of the things you have been taught"; 1:4). Luke then turns from a political event (the close of Herod's reign) to religious events (concerning an elderly priest and his wife and, in the next section, a carpenter and his young wife).

Zechariah was not the high priest or a chief priest; he was an "ordinary" priest of the division of Abijah. First Chronicles 24 describes the origin of the twenty-four-division system of priests. King David set the order of priests and Levites. Two groups of priests operated in the days of King David. They represented the sixteen priestly sons of Zadok and the eight priestly sons of Ithamar. Each of the twenty-four divisions was responsible, twice a year, for services in the temple.

In Jesus' time one high priest (an appointee of Rome), two hundred chief priests who represented the elite of Jerusalem, and about seven thousand ordinary priests who lived outside Jerusalem served in the temple. These ordinary priests were separated into twenty-four divisions. Their responsibility was to choose by lot several of their group who would serve at separate priestly tasks. Zechariah's task was attending to the offerings of incense and unleavened bread. Another priest would kill the sacrificial animals. Others were to light the sacred altar fires. The burning of incense was a symbolic act of offering prayer in behalf of all Israel. The placing of fresh goblets of wine and unleavened bread (the bread of the Presence) was symbolic of the communion between the believers and their Lord God. The priest's concluding action each day was to offer the ancient benediction found in Numbers 6:24-26, "The LORD bless you and keep you. . . ."

Zechariah was chosen by lot from the eighth of twenty-four divisions; his division was named Abijah. He served the Lord for a week, serving in the wonderful Holy Place. As a priest, he had to be a fully accredited descendant of Aaron.

Zechariah's wife had been barren throughout their long marriage. Perhaps at Elizabeth's urging, Zechariah, while renewing the bread of the Presence and offering the symbolic prayers for all Israel via incense, dares to pray for his wife. Somewhat like Moses, who saw the "angel of the LORD" in the bush (Exodus 3:2), so Zechariah experiences "the angel" while he serves at the altar that day. *Fear* is an idiom for *awe* or religious experience. The angel tells the sincere priest that his wife will bear a son whom Zechariah is to name John.

Zechariah doubts that he and Elizabeth can have a child, since they are old. Because of Zechariah's doubts, the angel (Gabriel) says he will becomes speechless and remains so until eight days after John's birth.

Zechariah's inability to pronounce the benediction on all the worshipers must have disappointed him and them too. But by signs he indicates that he has experienced the living God in his life. The crowd understands that he has had a vision of God. Then Zechariah goes home to Elizabeth. She conceives and bears John.

Luke 1:26-56. When Elizabeth is six months pregnant, Mary receives an announcement from God, by way of Gabriel, that she too will bear a male child, whose name will be Jesus. In Jesus, God has been and is with us, always. "The Word became flesh and made his dwelling among us" (John 1:14). God became incarnate in Jesus. Note that Mary also asked Gabriel, "How will this be?" While we can't know, perhaps her youth and inexperience were the reasons for a detailed response, which was denied the older, more experienced priest Zechariah. While John's birth carries great significance, we might also speculate that Gabriel's elaboration ensured that the even greater good news of Jesus would be clearly known, anticipated, and heralded.

Luke 1:35 calls to mind Genesis 1:2, where the Spirit of God hovers over the waters, bringing life into being. A child is being born of Mary, who is set apart by God.

Mary leaves Nazareth to visit Elizabeth, her relative. On meeting, both know that each is bearing a son of great significance. Both Mary and Elizabeth know the experience of being "filled with the Holy Spirit." Mary and Elizabeth mark the beginning of God's new action in humanity's behalf.

Mary praises God. She breaks into song: "My soul glorifies the Lord." The song is known as the *Magnificat*, which comes from the first word in the Latin translation of this song. Mary, who is three months pregnant, stays three months with Elizabeth, probably until the baby John is born.

Luke 1:57-80. Eight days after a Jewish boy is born, the parents mark their son as a son of Abraham by circumcision. At this time a Jewish boy also receives his name. This ritual was performed for John and later for his cousin Jesus.

Many of Luke's sources probably go back to oral traditions that were perhaps written down later by loving persons for memorization by others. One could easily mix two independent and significant poems, especially eighty years after the event. Such seems to be the case with the words Zechariah quotes as prophecy: "He has raised up a horn of salvation for us / in the house of his servant David" (1:69). Zechariah clearly is singing about the birth of Mary's son Jesus. (Jesus is descended from David; John is descended from Aaron.)

On the other hand, 1:76-77, 80 clearly refers to John, who will baptize thousands unto repentance and forgiveness of their sins. Luke 1:68-75, 78-79 refers to Jesus, who will bring light into the darkness of this world.

Luke 2:1-20. Luke likes order; so he gives dates, as well as names of significant persons and events. He states that Augustus Caesar (Roman emperor, 27 BC–4 BC) has given orders for a general enrollment of all persons in his empire. This enrollment took place, notes Luke, when Quirinius was governor of Syria. Against the background of royalty, Luke focuses on a simple carpenter and his wife—Joseph and Mary—the birth of whose baby is imminent. Finding no room in the inn, they go to a stable, where their son is born.

Read Exodus 33:14 aloud; then discuss how the shepherds fulfilled this experience that night. God has come very near; indeed they could say they had felt God's presence. God had been with them. Emmanuel! Had they not heard the angels proclaim, "Glory to God in the highest heaven, / and on earth peace to those on whom his favor rests"?

Not long after, they kneel at the manger where the baby Jesus, the one to be Lord Jesus Christ, lies. The heartstrings of the shepherds vibrate with the frequencies of the harp strings of the heavenly host. "The shepherds returned, glorifying and praising God." And Mary treasures all these things, knowing that what she teaches Jesus will be spiritual muscle and sustenance as her little boy grows to manhood.

Luke 2:21-52. After Jesus' circumcision and naming, two other ceremonial rites are needed. The fortieth day after birth, Mary receives her ritual of purification (Leviticus 12:2-4). Then the parents present the baby to God, who ordered Moses to consecrate to God all the firstborn children and animals of all the people of Israel (Exodus 13:2). To this day, Orthodox Jews dedicate their first son to study the law from ages four to twenty-one. This dedication to studying the law may be bypassed by making an offering of redemption—a lamb if one is wealthy or two turtledoves or two young pigeons if one is poor, as were Mary and Joseph. The aged Simeon, who has yearned for the day when his eyes can see the long-awaited Messiah, ecstatically declares the words of Luke 2:29-32.

Luke knows of no trip to Egypt; so the Gospel states, "They returned to Galilee to their own town of Nazareth" (2:39). There the boy Jesus developed in many fine ways (2:40).

Luke states that "every year Jesus' parents went to Jerusalem for the Festival of the Passover" (2:41). Jesus, at twelve, probably has visited the temple several times with his family and very likely has spent some time during these years with John, his cousin. They may have taken their bar mitzvahs together when they reached their thirteenth birthday. Each loved God and sought insights into the truths about Judaism and God's purposes for human life.

At their bar mitzvahs, they would naturally ask questions of the many priests in the temple. Jesus' and John's purpose was to listen to the elders, not to try to tell them truths the elders had not yet heard.

When Mary and Joseph leave Jerusalem for Nazareth, they discover after a day's journey that Jesus is not with them. Returning to Jerusalem, they find him with the priests, whose duties include instruction in the law. Mary asks Jesus if he did not know that she and his father were looking for him anxiously. Jesus replies, "Didn't you know I had to be in my Father's house?"

Luke reports that the child "grew in wisdom and stature, and in favor with God and man" (2:52).

DIMENSION THREE: WHAT DOES THE BIBLE MEAN TO ME?

The group may discuss the following questions or topic or use the material in the participant book.

Luke's Methodology of Writing

The first two chapters of Luke are a part of Luke's special contribution to Christianity. His Nativity scene is unique, differing from Matthew's. Let us seek several insights that this Gentile compiler and author offers us from the first several pages of his Gospel. His description in the preface of how his Gospel came into being is a major contribution to our understanding of the Bible. He states clearly that he sought various sources of information—written documents (such as the Gospel of Mark and a "booklet" of the teachings of Jesus), statements by witnesses who heard Jesus, and the testimony of various ministers of the word. From these varied sources he compiled his Gospel and the Book of Acts.

Without saying so, Luke assumed we would know that his Gospel would be as dependable and/or valid as his sources. Luke carefully collected, read, and often rewrote material he would print, as a good editor does today. He knew God needed persons to write. He knew God needed inspired persons through whom the divine Spirit could work.

Ask participants to discuss their attitude toward this Gentile physician for having told how he compiled the third Gospel.

Ask participants to think about the spirit of Christmas and the songs they hear. What makes for a true Christmas spirit? Write the answers on a chalkboard, a whiteboard, or on a large piece of paper.

Angelic Promises

Luke points several times to angelic activity to accomplish God's purposes. Zechariah and Mary obviously believed in angels as God's agents and in that form of communication concerning God's purposes. Do you think angels still speak to individuals today? If so, what form might they take? How would one know that this being is an angel?

The angel Gabriel comes to both Zechariah and to Mary to promise them children. Both question him, asking, "How can this be?" What are the complexities that lead to the question for each person (Zechariah, Elizabeth, and Mary)? What is the nature of Gabriel's response, and why do you think it differed in kind for them?

The births of John and Jesus are spectacular, each in their own way. Imagine you are a neighbor and witness to each family. What does this make you think about the families? about God? about God's activity in the world?

A Precocious Child

Jesus had been conversing with the religious leaders, evidently, over the course of several days. What kind of questions would a confirmand of "just thirteen" ask today at his bar mitzvah or confirmation? If you had three days all to yourself to ask questions of Jesus, what might you ask?

The Spirit of the Lord is on me, / because he has anointed me / to proclaim good news (4:18a).

THE KEY TO JESUS' PUBLIC MINISTRY

Luke 3:1–4:30

DIMENSION ONE:
WHAT DOES THE BIBLE SAY?

Answer these questions by reading Luke 3

1. What two sets of dates does Luke give us for dating the ministry of John (and therefore Jesus' ministry)? (3:1-2)

    Luke gives the political date, the fifteenth year of the reign of Tiberius Caesar, and the religious date, during the high-priesthood of Annas and Caiaphas.

2. Where is John, the son of Zechariah, when the word of God comes to him? (3:2)

    John is in the wilderness.

3. Where does John go to preach? (3:3)

    John preaches in "all the country around the Jordan."

4. What does John preach? (3:3)

    John preaches "a baptism of repentance for the forgiveness of sins."

5. What does John say to the crowds who come to him? (3:7-9)

    John tells them that only repentance can save them, not just being Jews—having "Abraham as our father."

6. What responses does John make to three different groups that come to him? (3:10-14)

   He tells the multitudes to learn to share with those who have nothing, the tax collectors to collect accurately, and the soldiers to refrain from extortion and false accusation and to be content with their pay.

7. How does John respond to those who think he is the Messiah, the Christ? (3:15-18)

   John says, "I baptize you with water. . . . He will baptize you with the Holy Spirit and fire. His winnowing fork is in his hand . . . to gather the wheat into his barn."

8. Why does Herod the tetrarch imprison John? (3:19-20)

   John condemned the tetrarch's "marriage to Herodias, his brother's wife, and all the other evil things he [Herod] had done."

9. When John baptizes Jesus, at what point (before, during, or after) does Jesus experience heaven opening before him? (3:21)

   Jesus sees heaven open after he has been baptized and while he is praying.

10. To whom does the voice from heaven declare that Jesus is God's Son, "whom I love"? (3:22)

    The Holy Spirit (God), speaking from heaven, says to Jesus, "You are my Son, whom I love; with you I am well pleased."

11. How old is Jesus as he begins his ministry? (3:23)

    Jesus is about thirty years old.

Answer these questions by reading Luke 4:1-30

12. What leads Jesus in the wilderness? (4:1-2)

    Jesus is led by the Spirit for forty days.

13. After fasting forty days, Jesus is hungry and experiences three temptations. What are these temptations? (4:3-12)

Jesus is tempted (1) to turn stones into bread, (2) to assume authority and splendor over all the kingdoms of the world, and (3) to jump from the highest point of the temple to demonstrate his messianic power.

14. How does Jesus deal with these temptations? (4:4, 8, 12)
    Jesus quotes passages from the Hebrew Scriptures, what Christians now call the Old Testament.

15. After the forty days in the wilderness, where does Jesus go? (4:14)
    Jesus returns to Galilee.

16. Before going to Nazareth, where does Jesus teach? (4:15)
    Jesus teaches in several synagogues in Galilee.

17. Where would Jesus normally be on the Sabbath? (4:16)
    Jesus usually would be found in the synagogue, "as was his custom."

18. What is the scroll from which Jesus reads? (4:17)
    He reads from the scroll of the prophet Isaiah.

19. To what passage of Scripture does Jesus turn? (4:18-19)
    Jesus turns to Isaiah 61:1-2: "The Spirit of the Lord is on me, / because he has anointed me / to preach good news to the poor. / He has sent me to proclaim freedom for the prisoners / and recovery of sight for the blind, / to set the oppressed free, / to proclaim the year of the Lord's favor."

20. What does Jesus say that makes all speak well of him? (4:21)
    Jesus says, "Today this scripture is fulfilled in your hearing."

21. What is the congregation expecting Jesus to do? (4:23)

    They are interested not so much in what Jesus says, but that he do what he "did in Capernaum."

22. How does Jesus deal with his friends' prejudices? (4:25-27)

    Jesus reminds them of how God, during a long and severe famine, did not give help to any Jewish women but fed a widow in the region of Sidon; also, God did not cure any Jewish leper, but he did cure a Syrian leper.

23. What do the worshipers do to Jesus? (4:28-29)

    They drive him out of the town, take him to the brow of a hill, and try to throw him off the cliff to kill him.

24. How does Jesus escape? (4:30)

    Jesus "walked right through the crowd and went on his way."

DIMENSION TWO:
WHAT DOES THE BIBLE MEAN?

The Scripture for this lesson, the beginning of Jesus' Galilean ministry, is divided into four themes:

    1. The Message of John the Baptist (3:1-20)
    2. Jesus' Baptism and His Genealogy (3:21-38)
    3. The Temptation of Jesus (4:1-13)
    4. Jesus' Declaration of His Messiahship (4:14-30)

Luke 3:1-20. As we learned in Luke 2:1, Luke wants to be as precise as possible where events and dates are concerned. In these verses Luke gives two sets of dates, one based on the secular political leadership, the other based on religious leadership.

The dates based on the political leadership are drawn from three groups: the Roman emperor, the governor of Judea, and three tetrarchs (rulers of nearby regions). The first political leadership is the emperor, Tiberius Caesar (AD 14–37), who succeeded Augustus Caesar. During the fifteenth year of Tiberius's reign, John the Baptist begins his ministry.

The second political leadership is Pilate, who was governor of a province that included Judea, Samaria, and Idumea. Pilate held office from AD 26 to 36. The third political leadership is the three sons and successors of Herod the Great: Herod Antipas (tetrarch over Galilee), Philip (tetrarch of Iturea and Traconitis), and Lysanias (tetrarch of Abilene—a country west of Damascus). A tetrarch is one who rules one-fourth of a kingdom. You may want to point out these areas on a map of Palestine, showing their relation to Judea. Jesus was a political subject of Herod Antipas.

The religious set of dates refers to Annas and Caiaphas. Annas headed one of four powerful clans of high priests who were not descendants of Aaron but who purchased their position from Rome. The high priests were appointed by the Roman emperor. Annas had been high priest from AD 6 to 15. Caiaphas was appointed to serve as high priest from AD 18 to 36.

Luke notes that John, son of the priest Zechariah, is in the wilderness when the "word of God" comes to him. Some scholars assume John was at Qumran, in the southern part of the wilderness of Judah. If so, he may well have been a member of the Essenes, a dedicated priestly group who expected the kingdom of God to come suddenly at any time. The major expectation of this group was the coming of the long-awaited Messiah, who would come from the heavens with a great military force of angels to destroy the Roman military force of occupation and establish the kingdom of Israel, with the Messiah as king.

John "went into all the country around the Jordan, preaching a baptism of repentance for the forgiveness of sins." Both Mark and Luke refer to Isaiah 40:3-5. They identify John's ministry with the "voice of one calling in the wilderness / 'Prepare the way for the Lord.'" The original cry was from the prophet in Babylon, about 587 BC–539 BC, who sought to revive his friends in exile and to ready them physically and spiritually to return home. The crooked shall be made straight, and the rough ways shall be made smooth—the prophet meant this literally, though John and Christians have taken it to mean becoming morally and spiritually straight. Truly, God is interested in that kind of reformation; for of such is the kingdom of God.

Group members might like to know that some scholars believe that verse 3:4b ought to read as follows:

The voice of one crying:

In the wilderness prepare the way of the Lord.

In this form, the verse more closely resembles Isaiah 40:3. Ask group members what difference this change makes. What was going on in John the Baptist's mind to make him address the crowds, "You brood of vipers! Who warned you to flee from the coming wrath?" The following scenario may help us understand John's strong feelings.

Luke 3:7-17 suggests the summer season when farmers are harvesting their grain. The crowds from Galilee and Judah have passed many such scenes as they walk toward the southern part of the Jordan River where John is preaching.

The travelers watch the process of harvest. Farmers have cleared circular areas on hilltops down to the solid limestone. The farmers place sheaves of barley or other grains inside the circle. If the farmer owns oxen, these animals move around the circle while pulling a small sledge with sharp spikes. The horn or rock spikes soon make a mass of chaff and grain. Next, the grain is separated from the chaff. Using a pitchfork, the chaff and grain is thrown into the air. The wind blows the chaff away. The grain falls to the ground and is swept into piles.

The chaff is swept into other piles and is eventually burned. At the burning, snakes and other vermin crawl out of the fiery pile, trying to escape. This scene may be behind John's harsh words (3:7-9). Kindness and subtle parables are missing.

Matthew 3:7 refers to the crowds of Luke 3:7 as Pharisees and Sadducees. They are the religious teachers who have come from Jerusalem to listen to the now-famous preacher. For these well read, ritualistic religious elite, John has harsh words. The harvesting scene seems appropriate: They are like snakes trying to escape the fires that burn the chaff. They say to themselves, *Our lineage is right; we are sons of Abraham, and by that fact we will be saved*. But John shouts out, You are saved not by the roots but by the fruits of your life. Salvation comes not by lineage but by your style of life.

So John calls them to repent of their lack of justice, compassion, and mercy. He applies these categories to three groups that come to him. The crowds (possibly referring to overly zealous Pharisees and Sadducees) are to learn to share what they have with those who have not. Tax collectors (those who are at the customs offices) are to be just and not extort larger fees than the law permits. Soldiers in the army of occupation are to maintain peace and to abide by the legal and just use of power.

The Essenes had no deep concern for social ethics; they felt the world was so bad that only God could redeem it by cataclysmic action. John's responses to the three groups suggest a severe weakness in his social ethics. He envisions no great emotional thrust for justice in the new era. He does not rise above the past.

John, as did Elijah, wears the hairy camel's skin garment (Matthew 3:4)—the symbol of a prophet. Through John the word of God is being expressed anew, and a greater prophet than he will speak soon. When the Messiah comes, he will baptize, not just with water, but with the Holy Spirit and with fire (the symbol for judgment).

John's "good news" is very limited, for his message is extremely limited—mostly to getting commitments through fear of judgment rather than through love. Jesus recognized John's personal commitment yet considered him the least in the kingdom of God (the new era).

Luke 3:21-38. However, Jesus left Nazareth and sought John out so he could be baptized. Surely these cousins spent many an hour together prior to baptism; so John could sincerely say, "I need to be baptized by you, and do you come to me?" (Matthew 3:14).

Yet Jesus insisted and was baptized with the crowds. *After* Jesus was baptized and while he was still praying, "heaven was opened." Help group members see the significance of Jesus' praying: He experiences Immanuel—God is with us—and the kingdom of heaven is opened. It was at this time that Jesus heard a voice from heaven saying, "You are my Son, whom I love; with you I am well pleased" (3:22). Certainly, this experience confirmed for Jesus that he was called of God to be the long-awaited Messiah (Christ).

Luke's genealogy of Jesus gives us the only statement as to his age: Jesus was about thirty when he began his ministry. It is interesting to know that priests had to be thirty before their ministry could begin.

Luke's genealogy differs considerably from that of Matthew. We note that Matthew goes from David through Solomon to Jacob the father of Joseph the husband of Mary. Luke reverses the order, stating that Jesus was "the son, so it was thought, of Joseph, the son [not of Jacob but] of Heli . . . [to] the son of Nathan, the Son of David . . . [and on to] Isaac, the son of Abraham . . . [on to] the son of Seth, the son of Adam, the son of God."

The two genealogies are in conflict, as has been known for some 1700 years. But their purpose is the same: to prove that Jesus was the Messiah, a descendant of David. Such was the popular expectation. Luke's list does not stop with David but goes to Adam, thus showing that God's interest is not just in the sons of Abraham (the Jews) but in all humankind. Thus Gentiles are included from the beginning of creation.

Luke 4:1-13. We have noted that after John baptized Jesus and while Jesus was praying, Jesus heard God express extraordinary pleasure in him as God's Son. Jesus' mind and spirit must have been greatly stressed as he realized God had anointed him the Messiah through John's baptism. His mind would have worked like flashes of lightning as he quickly thought of the many concepts of the Messiah.

Undoubtedly, Jesus had already disavowed John's view; for John sought a redemption only through God's action, not through anything human beings might do—not even as collaborators. All redeeming actions would come from God alone, not by any dedication of human efforts. There was no thought of God and humankind working together. This view supported an apocalyptic concept of the coming kingdom of God in which the angels of heaven fight against the demons and against demonic persons on earth.

The opposite view of redemption was to omit divine activity altogether and to assume that dedicated human efforts in social redemption would save the world and the people within it. This view was held by Zealots who were ready to fight to the death in order to clear Judah from all foreigners and other impure things.

The Pharisees and teachers of the law (the scribes) were waiting for a Messiah who would require and achieve total obedience to both the written laws (Torah) and the unwritten laws (verbal traditions). Obedience to all laws would change the lives of every participant. Jesus knew such legalistic obedience never made bad lives good, however. This concept of the Messiah, too, must be set aside.

The Sadducees, the priests such as Zechariah, also expected a messianic age—with the anticipation of One who would achieve full loyalty and obedience to priestly concerns related to the temple. The Messiah would emphasize and win full loyalty to observances of the three major religious festivals per year—the Feast of Tabernacles (Booths), Passover, and Atonement—plus sincere loyalty to minor duties such as making peace offerings, sin offerings, and paying various tithes. Jesus knew that the priestly kings of the Hasmonean period (immediately following the Maccabean wars, about 165 BC–163 BC) never achieved the kingdom of God. The priestly Essenes looked forward to One who would be prophet-priest-king.

In intuitive moments Jesus must have been aware that his mother Mary was touched, if not entered, by the Holy Spirit; the same was true of his relative Elizabeth (mother of John). Jesus experiences the Holy Spirit coming upon his life at baptism. This Spirit is now leading him into a forty-day wilderness retreat to meditate on his baptismal call to messiahship.

John wears the prophetic mantle (hairy garment) symbolizing the prophet Elijah. God is speaking through John in a new way. Psalm 74 is shattered by the new activity of the Holy Spirit. Is John the one who is to come? No! It is Jesus who is filled with the Holy Spirit. It is he who will baptize with the Holy Spirit at Pentecost!

A new era has come indeed. What kind of Messiah did Jesus conclude that God, not various religious groups, sought? It seems inevitable that Jesus, who loved his Scripture (what Christians now call the Old Testament), spiritually feasted on the servant passages (Isaiah 53 and 61:1-2) at his messianic banquet in the wilderness. How easily Jesus reads Isaiah 61:1-2 aloud at Nazareth. Here he explains what it means to have the Spirit of the Lord upon him. You might want to read these passages (Isaiah 53 and 61:1-2) to the group at this time.

Many Jews wanted and expected a prosperity-creating Messiah who would redeem his (Jewish) people from poverty and hunger. Many Old Testament passages support this hope. Other passages support a view that the Messiah will free his people from political (Roman) oppression. Other passages suggest divine healings will be the signs of his having come. Thus Jesus is tempted both by human and scriptural hopes. He decides that he will not administer a free food program; he will not turn stones into bread. (He knows that well-fed people do not necessarily make good people. People have a deeper hunger.) Jesus refuses to become a general of a military system that will coerce humankind to act with justice and righteousness. (Righteousness cannot be imposed by law, as Jeremiah learned.) Jesus refuses to obtain the accolades of humankind by performing miraculous acts. (People of all nations are easily won by astonishing feats, but these feats do not lead to spiritual conviction.)

Jesus quotes three passages from Deuteronomy (8:3; 6:13; 6:16), each of which nullifies one of his temptations, even though each might have contained some good. What each temptation proposes is good in itself, but it would keep Jesus from expressing and achieving his best. Jesus is loyal to the best, which he finds in Isaiah 53 and 61.

Luke 4:14-30. Luke begins this section by emphasizing the fresh activity of the Holy Spirit as Jesus goes to Capernaum and Nazareth. You might take time to point out on a map where these cities are located.

When Jesus speaks to his home congregation in the synagogue, the attending rabbi asks him to read the Scripture for the day and to address his friends. The rabbi would have followed the order of worship, which included singing a psalm, reciting the Shema (Deuteronomy 6:4-9), reciting the creed (of Deuteronomy 26:5-11), reading from the Torah and the Prophets (by a rabbi), sharing a psalm and a prayer, followed by the benediction (from Numbers 6:22-26). The reading that day was from the scroll of Isaiah. The attending rabbi hands Jesus the scroll, and he unrolls the scroll and reads 61:1-2. After handing the scroll back to the attendant, Jesus sits down.

After looking at each male member of the small synagogue, Jesus then proclaims, "Today this scripture is fulfilled in your hearing." He read the Hebrew lesson well and with rhetorical feeling. "All spoke well of him and were amazed at the gracious words that came from his lips" (4:22).

Luke greatly abbreviates Jesus' sermon, so let me expand it somewhat. First, every male in the auditorium would have said his daily prayers that morning. The prayers (from the Siddur, prayer book) contain these sentences: "Blessed art thou, Lord, our God, King of the universe, who hast not made me a slave. Blessed art thou, Lord our God, King of the universe, who hast not made me a woman."

In his first sermon Jesus includes a condemnation of this kind of prayer in a way that no man can help but understand. Subtly he raises his point: In the time of Elijah (850 BC) many widows in Israel suffered from the three-and-a-half-year famine, yet God sent Elijah to a woman from Sidon (she was a Syrophoenician—a Gentile—and a woman at that) to save her and her son from famine. Why should God have overlooked the Jewish widows? And Israel had many people with leprosy too, but God sent Elisha to heal the commanding officer of the Syrian army. Why did God overlook his real sons (of Abraham)? God healed Naaman, the commanding officer of the hated Syrian army. So how can you (Jews of Nazareth) thank God for not being a woman, and a Gentile woman at that? How can you thank God that you are not a Gentile (such as Naaman), and one with leprosy at that? Jesus' point is that God loves all persons—Gentile women as much as Jewish women and Israel's enemies (even lepers) as much as Jews.

Using the challenging verses of Isaiah 61:1-2, Jesus states how he knows the Holy Spirit is upon him: because he bears God's concerns for all persons. He is the Messiah because God has anointed him to preach good news to the poor, to proclaim release to all captives and recovery of sight to the blind, to set at liberty all those who are oppressed—and thus proclaim the new era, the kingdom of God. What a messianic mission!

Jesus' illustrations about God's concern for all persons shock the congregation. Yet no person dares say it is not biblical. It is good news—if you can take it.

As a result, they take Jesus out of the city and lead him to the brow of a high hill where they intend to throw him to his death. As they move along, Jesus walks with the men, probably calling them by name. I wonder, since he was not permitted to give the benediction at the synagogue, if he might have done so to various ones individually as they walked toward the brow of the hill? Then something unique happens, for Jesus soon reverses his steps and walks "right through the crowd and [goes] on his way." Are they ashamed? Encourage the group members to discuss this incident.

DIMENSION THREE:
WHAT DOES THE BIBLE MEAN TO ME?

The group may discuss the following topic and questions or use the material in the participant book.

John and Jesus

Consider the ministries of John and Jesus, Both preach repentance, both call out religious hypocrisy, both confront the "powers that be." Both are killed for their efforts, yet there is a difference in their approach. What are those differences, and what substantive difference did they make? They were close kin—cousins—and we might imagine them as childhood playmates. Why, do you suppose, was there not more clarity in John's mind about who Jesus is and what he intended to do?

Seeing the Messiah

Matthew, Mark, and Luke state that Jesus spends forty days in the wilderness with the devil (Satan), who tempts him in various ways. What kind of being is a devil? I find the record of Peter's confession at Caesarea Philippi helpful. (See Matthew 16:13-23; Mark 8:27-33; Luke 9:18-22.) Jesus asks who men are saying he is. Some say John the Baptist, others Elijah. Peter is the first disciple to say, "God's Messiah" (Luke 9:20). Jesus honors Peter by saying, "On this rock [the faith that Jesus is the Messiah] I will build my church" (Matthew 16:18). Jesus begins to explain the implications of being the Messiah—that he must go to Jerusalem and suffer many things. Peter rebukes Jesus, tempting him to change his plans of being God's kind of Messiah to being something less than the best (Matthew 16:22). This temptation is one Jesus faced in the wilderness, and it is a temptation that Luke hints at when he says the devil leaves him "until an opportune time" (Luke 4:13).

Peter and the disciples do not understand the kind of Messiah Jesus is. This fact is readily seen in Acts 1:3, 6, where Luke reports that after Jesus' resurrection, he teaches his disciples for forty days about the "kingdom of God." The disciples ask, "Lord, are you at this time going to restore the kingdom to Israel?" (1:6).

The disciples are still thinking in terms of a physical kingdom with its capital in Jerusalem, its throne built on the citadel of David, with armies, power, and authority. How can they be so blind? But they, as Peter, are not thinking the thoughts and ways of their Messiah. In this respect, they are devils. Jesus refers to Peter when he says, "Get behind me, Satan! . . . You do not have in mind the concerns of God, but merely human concerns" (Mark 8:33).

Many scholars assume Jesus used such a figure of speech to explain the psychological, moral, and religious stress under which he worked until he wholly dedicated himself to being God's Messiah, not a messiah dictated to or thought up by humans.

Jesus is dedicated to winning persons to God by persuasion, not by force; by love, not by fear; by strong and valid convictions, not by astonishing action on his part. In his loyalty to being God's Messiah, Jesus wins followers whose goals and mission in life are to fulfill those which Jesus adopted and shared with the people in Nazareth (Isaiah 61:1-2, in the spirit of the suffering servant of Isaiah 53).

Group members might value the opportunity to discuss private and church goals to see if they harmonize with those of our Messiah. If not, Jesus' charge to Peter may awaken us: "Get behind me, Satan!" This discussion could be the most important of our lives.

I have not come to call the righteous, but sinners to repentance (5:32).

JESUS' GALILEAN MINISTRY

Luke 4:31–6:49

DIMENSION ONE:
WHAT DOES THE BIBLE SAY?

Answer these questions by reading Luke 4:31-44

1. Where does Jesus go after he leaves Nazareth? (4:31)

    Jesus goes down to Capernaum, a city of Galilee.

2. While Jesus is in the synagogue, a man verbally accosts him. What is the man's problem? (4:33-34)

    The man is "possessed by a demon."

3. What does Jesus say to the demon? (4:35)

    "Be quiet! . . . Come out of him!"

4. Whose mother-in-law does Jesus cure, and what does she do after Jesus cures her? (4:38-39)

    Jesus cures Simon's mother-in-law of a high fever; she immediately arises and serves them.

5. Whom does Jesus heal? (4:40-41)

    Jesus heals those sick with diseases and those under the influence of demons.

6. Where does Jesus go the next morning, and what does he say he must do? (4:42-43)

    Jesus goes to a lonely place. He says he must go to other cities to "proclaim the good news of the kingdom of God."

7. In what country is Jesus preaching? (4:44)

Jesus is preaching in Judea.

Answer these questions by reading Luke 5:1-11

8. How many boats does Jesus see by the shore, and to whom do they belong? (5:2-3)

Jesus sees two boats belonging to fishermen.

9. From whose boat does Jesus speak? (5:3)

Jesus speaks from Simon's boat.

10. After teaching the people, what does Jesus tell Simon to do? (5:4)

Jesus tells Simon, "Put out into deep water, and let down the nets for a catch."

11. Why does Simon signal to his partners to bring their boat, and what are the results? (5:6-7)

Simon's nets are breaking from their load of fish. He calls his partners for help. Soon both boats are filled with fish.

12. What does Simon Peter do? (5:8)

Simon Peter falls at Jesus' knees and says to him, "Go away from me, Lord; I am a sinful man!"

13. Who are Jesus' first disciples? (5:10-11)

Jesus' first disciples are Simon [Peter], James, and John.

Answer these questions by reading Luke 5:12–6:11

14. What does a person suffering from leprosy beg Jesus to do? (5:12)

The leper begs Jesus to make him clean.

15. How does Jesus respond to the plea of the person suffering from leprosy? (5:13)

Jesus stretches out his hand and touches him.

16. What three things happen next? (5:13-14)
    Immediately the leprosy leaves the man. Jesus charges him to tell no one but to "go, show" himself to the priest for proof of his healing.

17. Why does Jesus forgive the sins of the paralyzed man? (5:19-20)
    Jesus forgives the man's sins because of his friends' faith.

18. Why do the teachers of the law and the Pharisees question Jesus' words? (5:21)
    The teachers of the law and the Pharisees believe that only God can forgive sin. Therefore, Jesus' words are blasphemous.

19. Who becomes the next disciple, and what does he do to honor Jesus? (5:27-29)
    Levi is the next disciple, and he gives a great feast in Jesus' honor.

20. What is Jesus' reply to the Pharisees and teachers of the law as to why he and his disciples do not fast? (5:33-34)
    Jesus replies, "Can you make the friends of the bridegroom fast while he is with them?"

Answer these questions by reading Luke 6:12-49

21. After a night in prayer, Jesus called his disciples and "chose twelve of them, whom he als0o designated apostles." Who are the Twelve? (6:12-16)
    The twelve disciples are Simon, Andrew (his brother), James, John, Philip, Bartholomew, Matthew, Thomas, James the son of Alphaeus, Simon the Zealot, Judas the son of James, and Judas Iscariot.

22. What are Luke's four Beatitudes? (6:20-22)
    "Blessed are you who are poor, / for yours is the kingdom of God.
    "Blessed are you who hunger now, / for you will be satisfied.
    "Blessed are you who weep now, / for you will laugh.
    "Blessed are you when people hate you, / when they exclude you and insult you / and reject your name as evil, / because of the Son of Man."

23. What does Jesus say about behavior toward enemies? (6:27-28)

    Jesus says, "Love your enemies, do good to those who hate you, bless those who curse you, pray for those who mistreat you."

24. What is the reward for this behavior? (6:35)

    The reward is that of being akin to God—"children of the Most High."

25. What is Jesus' test of goodness? (6:43-45)

    "Each tree is recognized by its own fruit," and "a good man brings good things out of the good stored up in his heart."

26. Everyone who hears and does Jesus' words is like a man who builds his house in a certain way. How does he build it? (6:48)

    He digs deep and lays the foundation for the house upon rock.

DIMENSION TWO: WHAT DOES THE BIBLE MEAN?

The Scripture for this lesson is divided into four themes:

  1. Healings in Capernaum, Time of Reflection (4:31-44)
  2. Jesus Makes His First Disciples (5:1-11)
  3. Healings and Confrontations (5:12–6:11)
  4. The Great Sermon (6:12-49)

Luke 4:31-44. When Luke says Jesus "went down" to Capernaum, he is referring to the fact that Nazareth is 1,300 feet above sea level and Capernaum is below sea level.

Capernaum was a strategic center for Jesus' ministry. It was a toll collection point and a major trade route from Egypt to Syria—"the King's Highway." It was a port for trade across the Sea of Galilee to the eastern shore, where Decapolis (Ten Cities) and Perea are found.

Josephus, an early Jewish historian, states that a synagogue was built in Capernaum by a Roman officer about AD 250. Probably Jesus preached in the synagogue whose foundations were those of this later edifice. Here the man with the impure spirit accosts Jesus.

"Go away" (4:34) translates a word of dismay: Oh me! The popular messianic hope of that day included healing of persons with both mental and physical illness.

We will face other exorcisms in this lesson. Notice the four characteristics of a typical exorcism story. First, the demon recognizes the exorcist and struggles to stay as he or she is. Second, the exorcist offers a command, which the demon seeks to evade. Third, the demon departs violently. Fourth, we receive a report on what happens to those who witness the freeing of the person who was under the influence of the evil spirit. Now reread (meaningfully) 4:33-37. Perhaps you will want to remind participants of Jesus' experience in Nazareth where the worshipers wanted to hear what he had done in Capernaum (4:23).

Verses 38-39 refer to Jesus' going to Simon's home. According to Luke, Simon is not yet a disciple. In a sense, Jesus is alone in his ministry.

When Jesus and Simon enter the house, they find Simon's mother-in-law with a high fever. At Simon's request Jesus goes to her. (Mark says he took her by the hand.) Jesus, standing at the head of the bed, rebukes the fever; and she is made whole (*shalom*—well, at peace, calm, healed). She then violates the law by serving them (Simon and Jesus). Only men served meals to men on such occasions. Jesus does not argue the point. She is grateful and wants to do something for him.

Soon Simon will be called to be a disciple. We wonder if his wife goes with him on his "missionary" journeys. Paul tells us that she did. (See 1 Corinthians 9:5.) We wish we knew the part the wives played in spreading the good news in many nations. Let participants consider possible roles the women played as they trudged the dirty roads for hundreds of miles.

Among Luke's many interests is Jesus' concern for women. Notice that the first miracle (4:31-37) is for a man; the second is for a woman (Simon's mother-in-law). Peter must feel some obligation to teach her, as well as his wife, about the healer who will before long become his Lord.

At the close of the Sabbath, sundown (6:00 p.m.) on Saturday, the physically sick and those under the influence of impure spirits or demons are brought to Jesus that their lives might be touched by the Master.

The next morning Jesus rises early and goes to a lonely place (Mark includes the words "where he prayed"). Remind group members again that Jesus has no disciples yet. He has crowds of people interested in him, but no disciples. The people seek Jesus and try to keep him from leaving them, but he refuses. Jesus tells them that he "must proclaim the good news of the kingdom of God to the other towns also, because that is why I was sent."

Luke 4:44 ends with Jesus teaching in Judea—a difficult concept, since he was and is teaching in Galilee. Jesus is interested in outreach. His outreach includes all of Palestine and beyond. It is interesting to notice that Luke uses the word *Judea* for all Jewish lands: Samaria; Galilee; even Idumea; and broader yet, Gentile lands and people from Syrophoenicia. God's kingdom is boundless. If group members ask for specifics about Judea's representing Palestine, you might post the following references: 1:5; 6:17; 7:17; 23:5; Acts 10:37. Luke may have thought that Mark's picture of Jesus' ministry (in Galilee and Judea) was too restricted.

Luke 5:1-11. Recall two events for this section of study. First, Jesus knows Peter and Peter knows Jesus—since Jesus has been staying in Peter's house for a while. Up to this time Jesus has no confidante, but he needs companionship in those higher levels of his thought life. Second, John 1:35-36 tells us that John the Baptist is standing with two of his disciples when Jesus walks by. John says, "Look, the Lamb of God!" (that is, the Messiah). The two disciples follow Jesus and listen to Jesus throughout the day. Andrew, one of the disciples, goes to find his brother Simon and brings him to Jesus. Jesus thus knows both Andrew and Simon.

"One day as Jesus was standing by the Lake of Gennesaret [the Sea of Galilee]," people crowd around Jesus to hear him speak. Being by the shore of the Sea of Galilee, Jesus takes advantage of a boat he sees moored nearby. Getting into Simon's boat, Jesus asks Simon to push him out to sea a bit, from which point he teaches the crowd on the shore. After Jesus finishes, he asks Simon to row out into the deep. Simon does, and they let down their nets. To Simon's amazement his nets start to break with the huge catch of fish. He calls to his partners to bring their boat near and share in the catch. Both boats are filled with fish. (John 21:11 reports Simon caught 153 fish.)

Simon Peter falls down at Jesus' knees in amazement and, taking the role of a sinner, asks Jesus to leave him. Notice that Simon does not move from awe to proclaiming Jesus the Messiah. This proclamation occurs at Caesarea Philippi many months later. Simon does see Jesus as a master miracle worker, but astonishment (as Jesus well knew) does not win converts to the Kingdom.

Even so, Jesus calls Simon and the other fishermen to "fish for people." Later they will be called to be apostles. The Codex Bezae (an ancient manuscript) translates verse 10, "Do not remain ordinary fishermen. Come and let me make you fishers of men!"

Luke 5:12–6:11. The Gospel of Luke records two stories of Jesus healing a leper. One of them is Luke 5:12-16. This description of being "covered with leprosy" suggests the disease was not Hansen's disease, which was loathed and feared, but some other skin ailment. Leviticus 13 describes "leprosy" in its many forms. The priests worked as health officers in these diagnoses, isolating victims and checking their conditions. (You might want to study Leviticus 13 and report to group members the varied symptoms and descriptions of skin diseases.)

Years ago I visited a leper colony at the southern foot of the Mount of Olives and was horrified by cases of Hansen's disease (which today is controlled but not conquered). Jews were taught to fear it "for their life." Mothers hugged their babies and ran after their children if a person with leprosy came anywhere near, seeking food or clothing. Jesus had been taught from infancy to respond with fear and even disgust, for people with leprosy were thought to have sinned against God in some terrible way.

Now Jesus, in the early days of messiahship, is faced with a man with leprosy. It must have startled him and recalled fearful moments when his mother had held him tightly to protect him from the presence and contagion of this dread disease. Jesus quickly deals with the fact that he is expected by law to stay away from lepers. Now one of these persons comes to Jesus and piteously cries, "Lord, if you are willing, you can make me clean." Jesus (possibly feeling the tug of his mother's prejudices and fear) reaches out and touches him, saying, "I am willing. . . . Be clean!"; and the man becomes clean.

Jesus tells the cured man, as Leviticus requires, to report to a priest and be proved clean. I can imagine the shout of joy, for I have heard such joy from a group of people suffering from leprosy when they were given clean sheets, pillows, and covers for the first time in many years. How Jesus, and God, must have rejoiced in the man's courage of conviction that brought the master's healing touch. Interestingly, after healing the man, Jesus withdraws to the wilderness for prayer.

We now turn to the healing of the paralyzed man (5:17-26). Mark (2:1-12) has the setting in Capernaum, in Peter's home where Jesus lived during his Galilean ministry. You might like to describe (or ask a group member to roleplay) Peter's feelings as the scenario moves through the destruction of the roof of the house. The house was probably a one-room house with an outside staircase leading to the roof. The flat roof was thatched with branches and straw and then covered with mud.

Apparently a group of Pharisees and teachers of the law (scribes and priests—Sadducees) have come from a number of villages of Galilee and Judea to observe the teacher, Jesus of Nazareth (Luke 5:17). Men come carrying a man who is paralyzed, hoping he can touch or be touched by Jesus. But the large crowd in the small room is an impossible barrier. So they make a hole in the roof and lower their friend. Jesus marvels at the faith of the men; and he tells the man, "Friend, your sins are forgiven." The teachers of the law and Pharisees, unconcerned about healing, say, "Who is this fellow who speaks blasphemy? Who can forgive sins but God alone?" Jesus listens and soon speaks on their level: "But I want you to know that the Son of Man has authority on earth to forgive sins. . . . Get up, take your mat and go home." Which the previously paralyzed man does! Little wonder that amazement and awe seize them all; and they say, "We have seen remarkable things today."

You might want to post the categories of miracle stories in Luke: (1) Exorcism, (2) Healing Stories (such as the paralyzed man), (3) Resuscitations, and (4) Nature Miracles. We will refer various healings to these categories as we study Luke's Gospel. In the miracle story of the man who is paralyzed, we may well have an example of psychosomatic (body-mind) healing. Sometimes illness is caused not by germs or a virus, but by selfishness, greed, hate, dishonesty, or uncontrolled passions. The sins of the mind cause debilitating illness as surely as do bacteria and germs. Jesus brings *shalom* (wholeness, health, peace) to those who respond to his offer of abundant life.

After leaving Simon's house, Jesus passes a tax collector named Levi (Matthew) sitting at his tax booth (5:27-32). Jesus calls him; and he follows Jesus, becoming one of the disciples. Levi invites Jesus and some tax collector friends to dinner, and Jesus accepts. The Pharisees and teachers of the law complain and question why Jesus should eat with such trashy (ritually unclean) people (5:29-30). Jesus tells these religious leaders that he came not "to call the righteous, but sinners to repentance."

The healing of the man with a shriveled hand (6:6-11) comes at the end of worship in a synagogue. Again, some Pharisees and teachers of the law watch, hoping to catch Jesus breaking their sacred traditions. Jesus knows their thought; malice is carved in their angry faces. In others Jesus can see and hear their yearnings to be clean and whole.

Luke 6:12-49. Luke 6:12-16 lists the names of the twelve disciples. Most of the Twelve are relatively unknown to us. In the compassion of these four Beatitudes (6:20-23), we have what Dante says of Luke, "this scribe of the gentleness of Christ."

1. "Blessed are you who are poor" (describing a basic characteristic of Christians, whose spiritual life is not determined by their material welfare), "for yours is the kingdom of God."

2. "Blessed are you who hunger now" (for a just and kind social order—right relationships), for your motives will set your mind in the paths toward justice.

3. "Blessed are you who weep now" over the painful consequences of uncontrolled sins (greed, hate, selfishness, dishonesty, inordinate passions), for you shall find enjoyment and relief from suffering.

4. "Blessed are you when people hate you" because of your stand for me and my way of life. Your reward is great in the spiritual life. Christians at the time of Luke's writing (about AD 80–85) faced the pain of being excluded from membership in many synagogues and of bearing the brunt of crude jokes and false statements.

What strategy can Christians employ to counter such evil persons? Jesus said, "Love your enemies, do good to those who hate you." (You might ask two group members to report on Mahatma Gandhi and Mother Teresa as outstanding persons whose lifestyles prove the validity of the strategy of love.)

Ask participants if they are ready to try an experiment. If so, state that Jesus' ethics reverse most ethical systems. Applying Jesus' ethics to our personal lives, ask group members to refer to specific situations that could illustrate one or two of Jesus' statements in 6:32-35.

Let the participants state in their own words the meaning of 6:35b. (For example, A Christian's character proves his or her kinship with the character of God; we are sons and daughters of God by imitating God's character.)

Ask if a person who is fundamentally ignorant of the valid directions of life (the "blind") can assume leadership in telling others the way to go; that is, "Can the blind lead the blind?" (6:39).

If a student, when fully trained, is like his or her teacher and the teacher is insensitive and opinionated, can his or her education be a success; or is it really a measure of the failure of both teacher and student?

On the other hand, a pupil (learner) who goes to Jesus and hears his words and does them is like a man who builds a house on a rock foundation; the house will never be shaken or destroyed by floods (6:47-49). A slight change of the metaphor would be, A person who builds his or her house of personality on the foundations of the Beatitudes and the love of God as seen in Jesus Christ has a structure that is everlasting; not even his or her death can destroy it.

DIMENSION THREE:
WHAT DOES THE BIBLE MEAN TO ME?

The group members may discuss the following topic or use the discussion topics above or in the participant book.

Healings

Jesus is the center of controversy for doing what today seems only like genuine compassion. If an ill, dying, or injured person is spared continued pain and is released from suffering, why wouldn't healing be appropriate? Most of the people noted in Scripture as being healed were in desperate straits—unable to work, sometimes separated from family and community, dependent on begging to get by. Think about the Pharisees' narrow response against the ongoing battles in the US about health care. If it is within our power to relieve suffering, what conditions MUST be satisfied first, if any? What makes those conditions important and to whom?

Luke 5:24—The Son of Man

We will consider one important issue: the meaning of the phrase *Son of Man*. *Son of Man* is the phrase that only Jesus used about himself (for instance, Luke 5:24). No other person in the Gospels refers to Jesus as Son of Man, yet Jesus himself uses it numerous times. What does the phrase *Son of Man* mean?

At the time of the Exile, the prophet Ezekiel used this phrase to refer to himself at least ninety times. The phrase referred to Ezekiel himself as God's agent to take God's message to his people. In the later years, Ezekiel prophesied hope—especially through the vision of the Valley of Dry Bones (Ezekiel 37). Daniel 7:13 says that "one like a son of man" will appear in the clouds of heaven before the "Ancient of Days" and will be given "authority, glory and sovereign power," representing the saints who will possess the Kingdom forever. The phrase, then, would have been quite meaningful to Jesus. The power of these references was very much alive in the thinking of the early church.

The healing in the home of Simon Peter of the man who was paralyzed (Luke 5:18-26) is the setting in which Jesus uses the phrase *Son of Man* for the first time. The phrase definitely has messianic overtones. Luke's two words "amazed" and "awe" (verse 26) were also messianic terms.

A typical alternate translation for *Son of Man* is "like a human being" (NRSV, for example). Does this mean that the Son of Man is like a human being, but not really a human being? is more than a human being, but in human form? is a human, but like a super-human being in terms of abilities, character, and accomplishments? something else? How does this term illuminate (or not) the role, character, and identity of Jesus as the Christ?

The blind receive sight, the lame walk, those who have leprosy are cleansed, the deaf hear, the dead are raised, and the good news is proclaimed to the poor (7:22).

4

JESUS: MESSIANIC TEACHER AND HEALER

Luke 7–8

DIMENSION ONE:
WHAT DOES THE BIBLE SAY?

Answer these questions by reading Luke 7

1. Who owns a servant who is at the point of death? (7:2)

A centurion has a servant who is "valued highly" and is "sick and about to die."

2. What does the centurion do to save the servant? (7:3)

He sends elders of the Jews requesting Jesus "to come and heal his servant."

3. Why do the elders help the centurion? (7:4-5)

They feel the centurion is deserving "because he loves our nation and has built our synagogue."

4. Why does the centurion send another delegation to Jesus, suggesting that he not come? (7:6b)

The centurion feels undeserving of having Jesus come to his house.

5. What does the centurion suggest instead? (7:7)

The centurion says, "Say the word, and my servant will be healed."

6. What happens? (7:10)

On returning home, those sent by the centurion to Jesus find the servant well.

7. As Jesus and a large crowd approach the city gates of Nain, what event is taking place? (7:11-12)
    They meet the funeral procession of a man who has died.

8. How does Jesus respond? (7:13-14)
    Jesus has compassion on the mother, a widow whose only son has died. Jesus touches the coffin; the bearers stand still; and Jesus says, "Young man, I say to you, get up!"

9. What does the crowd do and say after the man revives? (7:16)
    They are filled with awe and praise God, saying, "A great prophet has appeared among us."

10. What question does John the Baptist have two of his disciples ask Jesus? (7:19)
    "Are you the one [the Messiah] who is to come, or should we expect someone else?"

11. What happens "at that very time" that is a nonverbal answer to John's question? (7:21)
    "Jesus cured many who had diseases, sicknesses and evil spirits, and gave sight to many who were blind."

12. What is Jesus' verbal response to John? (7:22)
    Jesus says for the disciples to report to John what they have seen and heard about the persons who have been cured who were blind, lame, leprous, and deaf, and about the raising of the dead and the preaching of the good news to the poor.

13. What is Jesus' conviction about the importance of John the Baptist? (7:28)
    Jesus says, "Among those born of women there is no one greater than John; yet the one who is least in the kingdom of God is greater than he."

14. What kind of woman comes to Jesus while he dines as the guest of a Pharisee? (7:37)
    She is "a woman in that town who lived a sinful life."

15. What does she do that upsets the host? (7:38-39)

    She wets Jesus' feet with tears, wipes off his feet with her hair, kisses them, and pours perfume on them.

16. What does Jesus say in response to the woman's actions? (7:47)

    Jesus says, "Her many sins have been forgiven—as her great love has shown."

Answer these questions by reading Luke 8

17. What part do certain women play in the daily life of Jesus and his disciples? (8:1-3)

    These women help to support them financially "out of their own means."

18. In the parable of the sower, a sower sows his seed on four kinds of soil. What are these four kinds? (8:5-8)

    Some seeds fall along the path, some fall on rock, some fall among thorns, and some fall onto good soil.

19. Why does Jesus teach using parables? (8:9-10)

    Jesus says that the disciples are to know the secrets of the kingdom of God. For others he speaks in parables so that "though seeing, they may not see; / though hearing, they may not understand."

20. What is the purpose of good soil? (8:15)

    The good soil refers to "those with a noble and good heart, who hear the word, retain it, and by persevering produce a crop."

21. What is the purpose of a lighted lamp? (8:16)

    The lamp is put "on a stand, so that those who come in can see the light."

22. Who does Jesus say are his real relatives? (8:19-21)

    Jesus says, "My mother and brothers are those who hear God's word and put it into practice."

23. When Jesus rebukes his disciples during a great storm on the Lake of Gennesaret (Sea of Galilee), what does he ask? (8:25)

    Jesus asks them, "Where is your faith?"

24. After Jesus cures the uncontrollable demon-possessed man, what do the townspeople find the healed man doing? (8:35b)

    They find the man "sitting at Jesus' feet, dressed and in his right mind."

25. What happens to Jairus's daughter? (8:40-42, 49-56)

    Jesus raises Jairus's daughter from the dead.

DIMENSION TWO: WHAT DOES THE BIBLE MEAN?

The Scripture for this lesson about Jesus as a messianic teacher and healer is divided into four themes:

    1. Jesus Gives Life to Two Persons (7:1-17)
    2. Jesus and John the Baptist (7:18-35)
    3. Jesus and a Penitent Sinner (7:36-50)
    4. Jesus as Teacher and Miracle Worker (8:1-56)

Luke 7:1-17. Refresh your memory of Jesus' first sermon in Nazareth by rereading Luke 4:14-30 and the commentary on these verses from Session Two in this leader guide on pages 28–29. This story gives a biblical background for Jesus' interest in responding to a Gentile army officer who seeks God's healing ministry. Jesus assured the worshipers in Nazareth that God is interested in the needs of all persons, including a commanding officer of the Syrian army (Naaman), and that God sent Naaman to Elisha to be cured. Since the centurion is a "god-fearer," he probably has heard the story of Naaman read in the synagogue. (See 2 Kings 5:1-14.)

The centurion concludes that God, through Jesus, might save his servant. So he sends a delegation of Jewish elders to Jesus, asking him to come and heal his servant.

The elders tell Jesus that the centurion is worthy of anything Jesus will do for him, that "he loves our nation and has built our synagogue." Not far from the house, a delegation of the centurion's "friends" meets Jesus. They report the centurion's view of himself as unworthy (the opposite of the elders' report to Jesus), which indicates that this man of great authority has a strong sense of humility. The friends state that the centurion admits that he, like Jesus, is a man of authority. (The title *centurion* implies that he has authority over one hundred men.) The centurion observes that he represents and wields authority. People obey him when he gives an order. So (by analogy) Jesus represents and wields the authority of God. The centurion's request to Jesus, then, is not for Jesus to come to his house but simply to "say the word," and his servant (who is at the point of death) will live. The centurion's faith in what God can do through Jesus' speaking the word amazes Jesus. Jesus' emotional response is, "I tell you, I have not found such great faith even in Israel."

Participants may notice an interesting omission: Jesus does not say anything else, such as, "Be healed." Jesus simply admits that the man has more faith than any he has observed yet in Israel. Thus when the centurion's friends return to the house, they find the servant well. Luke's point is that Jesus' immediate presence is not required; he can heal from a distance equally well, and then, apparently by simply wanting it to be so. But more important than distance and any spoken words is the *faith* of the centurion. The servant lives through faith in action. To have faith is to recognize that God's power is also Jesus' power.

The raising of the widow's son takes place at Nain (7:11-17), a small village near Nazareth. Only Luke tells this story. If possible, locate Nain on a map for participants. Again, Jesus' actions parallel and evoke memories of the power of God exhibited in Elijah, who also ministered to a desperate Gentile widow.

As Jesus, his disciples, and a large crowd move toward the gate of the village, they meet a funeral procession. Luke focuses on the weeping mother, a widow, whose only son has died. In addition to the obvious pain of losing a child, a woman without a male relative as protector could be very vulnerable. Luke shows Jesus' compassion for the now childless widow by comforting her with the words, "Don't cry." At some point Jesus touches the coffin (he reaches out and stops the procession) and those carrying it stand still. During this pause, Jesus addresses the young man and says, "Young man, I say to you, get up!" And the young man sits up and begins to speak.

The people who witness this miracle glorify God and shout, "A great prophet has appeared among us. . . . God has come to help his people." Point out that the statement "God has come to help his people" is significant. Now what they can see in Jesus' miraculous resurrection of the youth is a "great prophet." The Jews have been looking for a prophet "greater than Moses," the Messiah; yet they fail to recognize Jesus.

Luke 7:18-35. In Luke 7:18-23, we have a bit of uncertainty, if not rivalry, on the part of John's disciples as they compare themselves with Jesus' disciples. John's disciples tell John what Jesus is teaching and doing. They wonder if Jesus is the Messiah. John is uncertain himself, so he sends two of his disciples to Jesus to ask him to clarify his work and mission. "Are you the one who is to come, or should we expect someone else?"

Recall that John is in prison, so he cannot go to see Jesus himself. During a brief period of time ("at that very time") Jesus' ministry illustrates (for the benefit of John's disciples) whether he is the Messiah. Jesus heals all kinds of diseases and plagues, exorcises evil spirits from many, and helps the blind to see.

Then Luke summarizes the facts that prove Jesus is the long-awaited Messiah, referring to Isaiah 29:18-19; 35:5-6; and 61:1-2. Ask group members to find Isaiah 35:5-6 in their Bibles. Read the passage. Then read the messianic passage from Isaiah 61:1-2. This passage is the same one Jesus read in the synagogue at Nazareth to help the people understand that the Spirit of God was upon him and that he was called to this prophetic ministry of messiahship. Jesus tells John's disciples, "Go back and report to John what you have seen and heard." John and Jesus have different concepts of what it means to be the Messiah and of what the kingdom of God is.

Jesus understands the Messiah to be the One who will fulfill Isaiah 61:1-2. Jesus believes in living a life of mercy, kindness, and unselfish service. Jesus tries to clarify this mission through his teaching. John based his ministry on judgment and obedience to moral law. Jesus' messianic action is not what John expects the Messiah to be doing. John is looking for the destruction of the morally unfit; Jesus is looking for the restoration of the unfit to moral health.

Jesus' statement, "Blessed is anyone who does not stumble on account of me," expresses his hope to John the Baptist and his disciples that they will not be offended by his (Jesus') lifestyle, his teachings, and his interpretation of what it means to be God's Messiah.

In Luke 7:24-35, Jesus (after the disciples of John leave) supports John's ministry. He asks some tough questions of those who previously listened to John in the desert: "What did you go out into the wilderness to see? A reed swayed by the wind?" The reed moves according to any wind that blows. One hardly thinks of John as a tender reed moving with any wind that blows! He is no easygoing, pussyfooting man. He is a hardheaded, demanding prophet. He is not a kind and indulgent man.

Is John a man clothed in luxurious clothes? Such men appear only in the courts of kings. That is hardly what John was at the Jordan, nor what he is now in his imprisonment. John is a prophet, with the austerity and uncompromising courage of a prophet.

Jesus adds, John is more than a prophet; he is sent by God to be a herald of a new day, fulfilling what Malachi envisioned: "I will send my messenger, who will prepare the way before me" (Malachi 3:1). John the Baptist is the forerunner (herald) of the Messiah; he is not Elijah returned as the Messiah. (See John 1:19-21.) He is a voice shouting, "Prepare the way for the Lord" (Luke 3:4).

John preached and baptized thousands of persons at the Jordan River. The common people especially responded to his ministry and were baptized. The Pharisees and teachers of the law heard John but refused to be baptized. Obviously, common people and religious leaders are in opposition. Many of the common people are for Jesus, and many Pharisees and teachers of the law are against Jesus.

It is possible that John has not thought of Jesus as Messiah until he hears about the impression Jesus makes. Two facts are obvious in the reading of this passage. John still has disciples, who remain aloof from the new movement of Jesus. And John does not preach the present kingdom that has arrived with Jesus. Therefore Jesus asks how he can compare these two groups of people. One group is happy and joyful; the other group is dour and sour, full of prejudice and empty of mercy. The two groups are like two groups of children: One group wants to play wedding and blow the flutes; the other group wants to play funeral and sing a dirge.

John's disciples prefer to play funeral hymns, fast, and drink no wine (7:33); but Jesus and his disciples are having a "wedding of a time," eating and drinking. Some call John too ascetic (austere, self-denying); some call Jesus a glutton, a drunkard, and a friend of tax collectors and sinners. What then shall we think of John?

Jesus says of John, "Among those born of women there is no one greater than John; yet the one who is least in the kingdom of God is greater than he" (7:28). John and his disciples live with judgment and fear; Jesus and his disciples experience the mercy of God and God's loving presence always.

Ask group members to read Acts 19 to see how Paul, when he goes to Ephesus, finds some disciples who have received "John's baptism." In what ways is this baptism incomplete?

In Luke 7:34, Jesus repeats a common criticism about himself when he says that he is "a friend of tax collectors and sinners." Apparently sinfulness is not a characteristic of eating and drinking as such. Some Jews find John too unsociable and Jesus too sociable.

Group members might profit from a discussion of the level of friendship that existed between John and Jesus. Both men were vitally interested in the kingdom of God. Yet they differed radically in their understanding of and approach to the Kingdom. Would they have spent much time talking together? Remind participants that John's message was not the gospel of his cousin Jesus. John held only to the Torah (the first five books of the Old Testament) as his Scripture. Jesus loved the writings of the prophets also, which he included in his Scriptures. John's major passage was from Deuteronomy 18:15—a greater prophet than Moses will come. Jesus loved especially the prophet Isaiah. John spent great amounts of time in the wilderness, a lonely, self-denying life. By contrast, Jesus loved to be with people and enjoyed friendships around the dinner table. Jesus tried to set people free. (You might ask two persons to roleplay the parts of John and Jesus, using the starter ideas suggested in this paragraph.)

Luke 7:36-50. These verses describe a story about Jesus, a Pharisee, and a woman who is probably a prostitute ("who lived a sinful life"). The Pharisee invites Jesus to dinner as his guest. Hearing about the dinner, the woman determines to attend the party too in order to show gratitude for Jesus' interest in people like her. She apparently is wealthy, for she takes with her an alabaster jar of expensive perfume to pour on Jesus' feet. (Compare a similar story recorded in Matthew 26:6-13; Mark 14:3-9; John 12:1-8.) Suggest to group members that each person analyze the character of the Pharisee and of the sinful woman. Then suggest that they analyze their own lives against those standards.

The Pharisee invites Jesus to dinner. Why? Out of friendship, out of gratitude, or out of a desire to be pompous and ingratiating? Why does he not greet Jesus with the usual kiss of a host, see that the dust is washed from his feet, anoint his head with perfumed oil, extend the normal courtesies of a host? What is going on in his mind? Why is the woman from the street there? The story does not suggest that she uses words of repentance for having sinned. But certainly many of her actions imply it. She bathes Jesus' feet with her tears (of joy or repentance?), wipes them with her hair, kisses his feet, and anoints them with her precious perfume. Though she says not a word, her actions speak louder than words. Jesus understands and interprets her actions correctly. She is expressing her love of and appreciation for him.

The Pharisee totally misunderstands the situation because he sees only an unclean woman of the street. The woman says not a word, but the Pharisee's thoughts condemn him. "If this man were a prophet, he would know who is touching him and what kind of woman she is." Jesus says, "Simon, I have something to tell you."

Jesus then tells the parable of a moneylender who has two debtors; one owes five hundred denarii, the other fifty. When the time comes to pay the debts, neither man can do so. The moneylender forgives them both. The question is, Which of them loves him more? Simon answers, "The one who had the bigger debt forgiven." Jesus approves Simon's answer and says, "Her many sins have been forgiven—as her great love has shown. But whoever has been forgiven little loves little." Jesus turns to the woman and says, "Your sins are forgiven. . . . Your faith has saved you; go in peace."

Luke 8:1-56. As Jesus goes through the cities and villages, preaching and bringing the good news of the kingdom of God, he is accompanied not only by the disciples but also by some women—Mary (of the fishing town Magdala on the west coast of the Sea of Galilee); Joanna (the wife of Chuza, Herod Antipas's household manager); Susanna; and many other women. These other women may well have been the wives of the disciples, who apparently traveled with their husbands. (See 1 Corinthians 9:5.) "These women were helping to support them [the disciples and Jesus] out of their own means." That is, they financed them while on their journeys. Probably these women assumed responsibility for preparing meals and making housing arrangements at night.

Luke 8:4-8, a parable of different soils, is intended to tell Jesus' audience about the quality of different hearers. What persons in an audience may hear (in sermons, lectures, classes) depends on the moral and spiritual quality of their lives. The quality of a person's life determines how much attention can be given to specific teachings, the level of possible reception, and the willpower to carry out the teachings.

The sower (the teacher or preacher) sows the seed. Some falls on hardened paths, is trampled on, and has no chance to grow. Some teachings fall on soil with a thin layer of dirt covering solid rock. Some teachings fall among thorns and are choked by those around them. And some teachings are sown in good soil (minds) and grow and yield a hundredfold. "Whoever has ears to hear, let them hear."

Luke 8:22-25 presents a nature miracle, the miraculous calming of a severe storm on the Lake of Gennesaret (Sea of Galilee). Equally important is that Jesus calms the fear in the hearts of seasoned fishermen and chides them for their lack of faith.

Luke 8:26-39 tells the story of another healing. The eastern shore of the Sea of Galilee is narrow and runs into very high and steep cliffs in the region of the Gerasenes. Here a frenzied man, who has been imprisoned and bound by chains from which he has escaped many times, apparently learns what has happened on the sea and in the boat. He hears that frightened men suddenly became calm and peaceful because one of their companions stood and spoke. That man spoke with authority to both storm and men. *Surely*, thinks the frenzied man, *he can help me.*

Luke describes a fascinating scene. As Jesus steps out of the boat, "Legion" (who is naked and has been living in one of the tombs) meets Jesus. Jesus recognizes his mental disabilities and orders the evil influences to come out of him. The man responds, "What do you want with me, Jesus, Son of the Most High God?" Jesus asks him his name. He replies, "Legion." (*Legion* is a military word for a division of six thousand men.) His name symbolizes his problem: Whenever he tries to make a decision, many contradictory voices cry out in his mind, wanting their answers to dominate all the others. His mind is a mob. Legion needs an integrating, centralizing power in his life. He finds that power when Jesus, in his messianic role, sets the prisoner free.

When villagers hear what has happened to the demoniac, they come to see this miracle. They find him "sitting at Jesus' feet, dressed and in his right mind; and they [are] afraid."

The two concluding stories of Luke 8 deal with a girl of twelve who is dying and a woman who has been sick twelve years (8:40-48).

The father of the girl is Jairus, "a synagogue leader." Judaism required at least ten men to form a synagogue. These ten men were known as the rulers or leaders of the synagogue. Jairus, having heard that Jesus is a healer, comes to request Jesus' healing power for his only daughter. "Please come and put your hands on her so that she will be healed and live" (Mark 5:23).

"As Jesus was on his way" to help Jairus's daughter, the crowd presses about Jesus. A woman in the crowd has suffered greatly because of a continual hemorrhage. This condition means she is ritually unclean, so she cannot worship in the Court of Women in the temple and is not acceptable to her husband. She suffers the pain of humiliation and presumed guilt of sin, not to mention the physical problem itself. Perhaps because Luke is a physician, he omits what Mark says about the woman: "She had suffered a great deal under the care of many doctors and had spent all she had, yet instead of getting better she grew worse" (Mark 5:26). She is desperate.

Perhaps Jesus might remove her uncleanness and restore her to a healthy relationship with God in the temple and with her husband, family, and friends. Twelve years of anguish force her to do what she certainly would not have done otherwise. She gets near the Master and touches his garment—perhaps only one of the four blue and white tassels (fringe) hanging from his outer cloak. (See Numbers 15:38-39; Deuteronomy 22:12.) She reaches out, touches a tassel of his garment, and is immediately healed.

Jesus stops short and asks, "Who touched me? . . . I know that power has gone out from me" (8:45-46). Trembling, the woman bows down at his feet and admits she has touched him. Jesus says, "Daughter, your faith has healed you. Go in peace."

While Jesus is still speaking, a man from the synagogue leader's house comes and says, "Your daughter is dead." Jesus tells Jairus, "Don't be afraid; just believe, and she will be healed." Jesus goes to the house, and with Peter, James, and John, plus the father and mother, he enters and says, "'My child, get up!' Her spirit returned, and at once she stood up." Again Jesus asks that they not tell others of this miracle. The time and the way of declaring his messiahship has not come.

DIMENSION THREE:
WHAT DOES THE BIBLE MEAN TO ME?

Giving Life and Healing

Jesus healed a servant at the brink of death, a man with severe mental illness, a woman who had suffered for years with hemorrhaging, and resuscitated a man and a little girl who had already died. In each case, he simply said the word, and they were well. If you were to witness a faith healer doing such things today, what would you think? What would you do? Have you ever wished for healing for yourself or for someone else that you approached God desperately in prayer, begging for relief? What happened? How did that influence your attitude and belief in God?

Penitent Sinners

After the woman bathed Jesus' feet with perfume, to the irritation of his host, Jesus told a parable about two debtors. One owed a debt of almost two months' wages and the other, about sixteen months' wages. One debt is large; the other huge. Both are unpayable and both are forgiven. In the parable, the one who owed more and was forgiven more, then "loved" more; that is, was all the more grateful. Do you think there are (or should be) degrees of forgiveness? of gratitude? Is there one standard for love and forgiveness for God, but a different standard for us (recognizing that we, of course, are not God)?

Luke 8:9-10—Insiders

Luke 8:9-10 and Matthew 13:10-13 are based on Mark 4:10-12, which suggests that Jesus teaches in parables so only "insiders" (disciples) will understand and respond to the message. Surely teaching only insiders is not Jesus' intention. Luke 8:16-18 emphasizes that a lamp is ignited for the sole purpose of shedding light. You do not put a lamp in a jar or under a bed, since no light can be shed to find your way. So it is with parables. Jesus tells parables to illustrate and explain by stories and metaphors that which otherwise is difficult to understand.

The Old Testament, through the survivors of the house of Judah (Isaiah 37:30-32), teaches the doctrine of the remnant. Not everyone responds to the call of God for repentance and new life. Only a few do so. Isaiah 6:9-10 deals with the theological difficulty of why some persons respond, but most do not. Inasmuch as God is ultimately responsible for all things, God then must be responsible for persons who do not see the light and refuse to accept God's truth. But Jesus does not believe in this doctrine of predestination. He clearly recognizes the freedom of persons to determine their own fate by their own choices.

The purpose of all parables is to let the truth be known. Truth is never willfully hidden. Parables are not secretive, they enlighten all. Early church leaders applied the doctrine of the remnant incorrectly to the parables of Jesus. True, many refuse, but not because the parables are obscure. People refuse because their minds are obstinate. Jesus teaches in parables in order that hearers might hear and be transformed.

"Who do you say I am?" Peter answered, "God's Messiah" (9:20).

5

THE DISCIPLES ACCEPT JESUS AS MESSIAH

Luke 9:1-50

DIMENSION ONE:
WHAT DOES THE BIBLE SAY?

Answer these questions by reading Luke 9:1-17

1. Before Jesus sends "the Twelve" on their first mission, what does he give them? (9:1)

Jesus gives his disciples "power and authority to drive out all demons and to cure diseases."

2. What does Jesus send them out to do? (9:2)

Jesus sends the disciples out "to proclaim the kingdom of God and to heal the sick."

3. What rules does Jesus give for their journey? (9:3-5)

They are to take nothing for their journey, to stay in one person's house, and to leave the town or house when they are not welcome.

4. What does Herod hear and think about these missions? (9:7-8)

Herod hears of all that is done—healing and preaching; but he is perplexed as to who their leader is.

5. What political leader "tried to see" Jesus? (9:9)

Herod, the tetrarch (ruler) of Galilee, wants to see Jesus.

6. After the disciples report to Jesus on their mission, where does Jesus take them? (9:10)

   Jesus withdraws with the disciples to a town called Bethsaida.

7. When the crowds search for and find Jesus at Bethsaida, where he and his disciples have withdrawn for a spiritual retreat, what does Jesus do? (9:11)

   He welcomes them, speaks to them of the kingdom of God, and heals their sick.

8. Late in the afternoon, what do the disciples ask Jesus to do? (9:12)

   They ask Jesus to send the crowd away so the people can find housing and food.

9. What does Jesus say to the Twelve? (9:13)

   Jesus tells them, "You give them something to eat."

10. After the disciples tell Jesus they have only five loaves and two fish, what does Jesus do? (9:14b-16)

    Jesus tells his disciples to divide the crowd into groups of fifty. He then takes the loaves and fish, looks up to heaven, and gives thanks for the food. Then Jesus gives the loaves and fish to the disciples to distribute to the people.

11. How many persons partake of this meal, and how much food is left over? (9:14a-17)

    Five thousand men (plus their wives and children) partake. Twelve baskets of broken pieces are left over.

Answer these questions by reading Luke 9:18-27

12. What responses does Jesus receive when he asks who people say he is? (9:18-19)

    Some people say John the Baptist; others say Elijah; still others say that one of the prophets has come back to life.

13. What response does Jesus receive when he asks, "Who do you say I am?" (9:20)

    Peter answers, "God's Messiah."

14. What command does Jesus then give the disciples? (9:21-22)

They are "not to tell this [that Jesus is the Messiah] to anyone." Jesus tells them that "the Son of Man must suffer many things and be rejected . . . and . . . be killed."

15. What must a person do to be Jesus' disciple? (9:23)

To be Jesus' disciples, persons must "deny themselves and take up their cross daily and follow [Jesus]."

Answer these questions by reading Luke 9:28-43a

16. Eight days later, what happens to Jesus on the mountain, where he goes to pray? (9:28-30)

"The appearance of his face changed, and his clothes became as bright as a flash of lightning." Moses and Elijah appear "in glorious splendor" and speak with Jesus.

17. Who does Jesus take to the mountain with him? (9:28)

Jesus takes Peter, John, and James with him.

18. What proposal does Peter make to Jesus? (9:33)

Peter proposes to make three shelters, "one for you [Jesus], one for Moses and one for Elijah."

19. What is the significance of the cloud? (9:34-35)

A voice speaks to the disciples from the cloud saying, "This is my Son, whom I have chosen; listen to him."

20. When the voice (of God) finishes speaking, who is left on the mountain? (9:36)

Jesus, Peter, John, and James are left alone on the mountain.

21. When Jesus, Peter, John, and James come down the mountain to the valley, who meets them? (9:37-39)

A large crowd and a father whose son has convulsions meet them.

22. Who has tried to heal the boy suffering from convulsions? (9:40)

    The disciples have tried, but they cannot.

23. What does Jesus do? (9:42b)

    Jesus rebukes the impure spirit, heals the boy, and gives him to his father.

Answer these questions by reading Luke 9:43b-50

24. While everyone is "marveling at all that Jesus did," what prediction does Jesus make of his Passion? (9:44)

    Jesus says, "The Son of Man is going to be delivered into the hands of men."

25. While Jesus tries to inform his disciples about his interpretation of the messianic hope, in what argument do the disciples engage? (9:46)

    The disciples argue "as to which of them would be the greatest."

DIMENSION TWO: WHAT DOES THE BIBLE MEAN?

The Scripture for this lesson, describing when, where, and how the twelve disciples finally accept Jesus as the Messiah (Christ), is divided into five themes:

1. Jesus Directs His Disciples in Mission (9:1-11)
2. The Feeding of the Five Thousand (9:12-17)
3. Peter's Confession and the First Prediction of Jesus' Passion (9:18-27)
4. The Transfiguration and Curing a Boy With Epilepsy (9:28-43a)
5. The Second Prediction of Jesus' Passion and a Pagan Exorcist (9:43b-50)

Luke 9:1-11. Inasmuch as Jesus is aware of his call by God to be the Messiah and inasmuch as he knows his Scripture very well, he cannot help but be influenced by Deuteronomy 18:15. This passage states that a prophet like Moses will come and that the people should listen to him. Jesus would have heard from childhood days how Moses served God yet was denied the right to enter the Promised Land. Jesus would have known the story of Moses' approaching death and how his successor (Joshua) was chosen and commissioned. (Read Numbers 27:15-20 to participants. Ask if they think this passage may have influenced Jesus in the commissioning of his twelve disciples.)

Some facts from Numbers 27:15-20 that participants may want to know are these: (1) Moses asks God to "appoint someone over this community." (2) This person shall be a shepherd to Israel.

(3) Joshua is called by God, for in him "is the spirit." He will be commissioned by Moses.
(4) After Moses commissions Joshua as his spirit-led successor, Moses is to "give him some of [his] authority."

Joshua is told to take twelve men from the tribes of Israel, one from each tribe. These twelve will lead Israel in their campaigns to conquer and win the land. How similar is the commissioning of the Twelve Jesus chose? (Read Luke 9:1-2 to participants, which tells how Jesus called the Twelve, investing them with his power and authority.) Joshua called for leadership to lead in a war that would obtain the Promised Land. Jesus called for leadership that would win the minds and attitudes of all human beings. The methods of Joshua and Jesus were poles apart. Joshua did not go out to convert people to the kingdom of God; Jesus sought to win persons to the kingdom of God by persuasion, not by coercion. So Jesus calls, trains, and sends out twelve "missioners" who will seek by way of teaching, healing, and exorcism to set the captives free, to help persons who are blind to open their moral and spiritual eyes and see, to know the day of the Lord is upon them (Isaiah 61:1-2).

Though successful in teaching in Capernaum, Jesus apparently considers his work in Nazareth a failure. He leaves Nazareth and goes "around teaching from village to village" (Mark 6:6b). He would have gone to such villages as Nain (six miles southeast of Nazareth) and perhaps north to Sepphoris.

With the commissioning of the Twelve to represent Jesus' mission, we understand why he chose them and why Jesus prayed so earnestly in choosing them. Instead of being disciples who listen to his teachings, they now become preachers of his mission. His work becomes twelve times more effective.

Before commissioning the Twelve, Jesus gives them two important gifts: power (*dunamis*) and authority (*exousia*). The two Greek words, *dunamis* and *exousia*, also mean personal force and official right. The most effective leaders are those who possess both.

The commissioning includes five parts: (1) Jesus gives his own power and authority over all demons (impure spirits; Mark 6:7) and the power to cure diseases. (2) Jesus commissions them to preach. (3) Jesus gives them a rule for their journey: Travel light; take no staff, no suitcase, no bread, no money; take only one tunic (undershirt). Sandals were evidently allowed (Mark 6:9).
(4) Choose the house (the inhabitants are likely to be converts) and stay in that one place.
(5) If the people (town or family) do not receive you well, when you leave, shake off the dust from your feet. This latter suggestion is a rabbinic custom. When returning from a trip to a foreign land, such as Samaria, the rabbi would shake off any dust as a symbol that he wanted nothing of paganism attached to him.

Apparently the ministry of the twelve disciples was very successful, for even Herod the tetrarch heard of "all that was going on." Ask group members what "all that was going on" might mean for Herod Antipas. (Consider specific healing miracles; unique teachings of and about Jesus; exorcisms by the disciples, such as setting people free from their mental and spiritual uncleanness; and so forth.)

Ask group members to suggest the ways in which Herod would have heard the gospel and ways he did not. For example, Herod lived in a time when there were no radios, no television sets, no satellite communication systems, no newspapers, no social media. He was totally dependent on oral (vocal) communication. Herod listened to those who either gossiped or had heard. (For example, do you think Chuza, husband of Joanna, who helped finance Jesus (8:3), might have reported about his wife's experiences? Could Chuza have spoken plainly in an official meeting?)

Herod is "perplexed," in part because some have told him that Jesus is John resurrected—Herod's beheading of John has been on his conscience for some time. Herod promised Salome (Herodias's daughter by Philip, Herod's half-brother) to grant any request she made. He obviously could not break his word. A promise is a promise—especially when the high-ranking military officers, mayors of villages and cities, and representatives from Rome have come for the birthday party and are witnesses. (Discuss this question: Is Herod unique in keeping promises that many persons hear but being unconcerned about keeping promises that are private?)

Since John the Baptist's beheading, Herod has been hearing great and grave reports about Jesus and his twelve disciples. Many have just finished a mission in several of his cities where they preached, healed diseases, and exorcised impure spirits in the name of their teacher, Jesus (9:6).

Herod's question "Who, then, is this I hear such things about?" is the question of the various episodes of this lesson. The man, Jesus, whom Herod hears about, sends disciples to preach throughout Herod's kingdom. Jesus feeds 5,000 men at one sitting. His disciples hear Jesus admit for the first time that he is the long-awaited Messiah. Peter, John, and James see Jesus transfigured on a high hill as he prays—and is ministered to by Moses and Elijah. He heals a boy from his seizures. He now moves toward Jerusalem. Herod has asked rightly, Who is this man? We will look more closely at the scenario.

Luke 9:12-17. Ask class members if Jesus knew and loved his Bible (what Christians now call the Old Testament). Must we not assume that he did? Jesus would have known well an experience in the life of the "sons of the prophets" during the terrible famine when Elisha was their head. One hundred prophets were without food. "A man came from Baal Shalishah, bringing the man of God [Elisha] twenty loaves of barley bread baked from the first ripe grain, along with some heads of new grain. 'Give it to the people to eat,' Elisha said. 'How can I set this [little bit of food] before a hundred men?' his servant asked. But Elisha answered, 'Give it to the people to eat. For this is what the LORD says: "They will eat and have some left over."' Then he set it before them, and they ate and had some left over, according to the word of the LORD" (2 Kings 4:42-44).

Jesus referred to a miracle by Elisha when he preached in Nazareth, but the people refused to listen (Luke 4:16-30). Now Jesus addresses a similar question to his apostles, who have completed their mission throughout the villages of Galilee and have listened with five thousand men as Jesus taught all day. They are at Bethsaida, where Jesus invited the Twelve to spend the day in sharing their new experiences as teachers and healers (their first mission). The crowd comes and interrupts Jesus' plans for spiritual renewal of his disciples. He never shows disappointment at this interruption of his personal plans. He welcomes the people.

The order Jesus gives to his disciples is this: "You give them something to eat." The disciples can only respond with despair: "We have only five loaves of bread and two fish." As with Elisha, how can you feed one hundred hungry men on twenty loaves? How do they feed five thousand men and their families on that which would be inadequate even for a man and his wife?

Jesus orders the disciples to divide the crowd into groups of approximately fifty each. After the inevitable commotion of dividing into groups, he makes them all sit down.

Jesus takes the five loaves and the two fish; looks up toward heaven; and blesses (that is, praises God) and breaks them, giving them to the disciples. Then the disciples move among the groups, serving those who need food. (You might ask which of the Synoptic Gospels states how Jesus multiplied the fish and loaves to serve the great crowd. The answer, of course, is none; multiplication is not mentioned.) The people eat and are satisfied. And they (the disciples who served) take up what is left over, twelve baskets of broken pieces.

The early church's *Eucharist* (a Greek word meaning, even today, thanksgiving) had the same steps that a bishop or elder uses to administer Holy Communion, or the Lord's Supper. The people sit; the leader takes the bread, blesses and breaks it, gives it to the people, and takes up the broken pieces. Many biblical scholars assume that Luke's account is influenced by the way the Lord's Supper was served at the time Luke wrote his Gospel.

Your group members might like to know that drawings of bread and fish appear on frescoes in the catacombs symbolizing the Lord's Supper. It is interesting that Jesus is at Bethsaida, which means "house of fishing," when the dinner of fish and bread is served.

Describe the setting for the feeding of the five thousand. The crowd has come to the area of Bethsaida, where Jesus and his disciples held a brief and interrupted retreat. Jesus welcomes the crowd and teaches them. Jesus always emphasizes the love of God with its overtones for moral action—sharing what you have with those who do not have, the meaning of Christlike human relationships based on justice and good intentions, the divine thrust in human lives urging us to yearn for and accept Jesus' lifestyle that will result in peace. (Perhaps you could let group members suggest a number of other emphases Jesus would normally raise.)

You may want to refer to what scholars call "the big omission" in Luke's Gospel. Between Luke 9:17 (the end of the account of the feeding of the five thousand) and 9:18 (the beginning of Peter's confession at Caesarea Philippi) are two large groups of material in both Matthew and Mark: Matthew 14:22–16:12 and Mark 6:45–8:26. We do not know why Luke omitted these episodes, unless he felt they would interrupt the pursuit of Herod's major point: Who is this man, Jesus?

Luke 9:18-27. Luke's choice of materials for this chapter concentrates on the identity of Jesus. Peter is the first of the Twelve to state forthrightly that Jesus is the Messiah. Both Mark and Matthew tell us that Jesus and his disciples go to Caesarea Philippi. Luke does not refer to Caesarea Philippi, perhaps thinking it does not matter where the great event takes place.

This Scripture passage introduces a new element in Jesus' ministry. At this point in Mark's Gospel, Jesus is no longer viewed as a public figure. Rather Mark portrays Jesus as the fulfillment of Isaiah's prophecy of the suffering servant. Jesus is portrayed as seeking to prepare his disciples for his Passion—for his abuse and his suffering on the cross. In Luke we shall see Jesus continuing his public ministry through what scholars call the Lukan Insertion (9:51–19:27).

Jesus and his disciples have been moving northward, in part to leave Galilee (ruled by Herod Antipas, who has said he would like to see Jesus) and in part to be alone together as Jesus teaches them the meaning of messiahship. As Jesus prays in the hilly area of Caesarea Philippi, he turns to his disciples and asks them who the people say he is. Do they know his identity? The disciples answer that some people say he is "John the Baptist; others say Elijah; and still others, that one of the prophets of long ago has come back to life." Now Jesus asks his disciples the question Herod has been asking: "But what about you? . . . Who do you say I am?" Peter answers, "God's Messiah."

Up to this point, when persons are healed or set free from unclean spirits and have declared that Jesus is the Holy One and the Son of God, Jesus asks them not to tell anyone. Now Jesus wants his disciples to recognize him as God's "beloved son," the Christ, the Messiah. Jesus accepts Peter's confession but declines to make it public. Jesus needs time to reinterpret the popular concept of Messiah (which most of his disciples hold) in terms of loving service, suffering, and sacrifice. His chosen men do not like this view.

Ask participants to discuss Jesus' command to his disciples at this time, to tell Jesus' identity to no one. What would it have hurt? Were the disciples free to discuss it? How long did Jesus want to wait and for what reason? (Jesus will wait until Palm Sunday, when he will demonstrate Zechariah's understanding of one who would come riding on a lowly colt rather than a military stallion and "'not by might nor by power, but by my Spirit,' says the LORD Almighty" (Zechariah 4:6).

The significance of the phrase "the elders, the chief priests and the teachers of the law" lay in the fact that this group forms the Sanhedrin in Jerusalem. They are the final court of appeal for Jews in Jerusalem and throughout the land. Jesus now predicts, for the first time, that he, the Son of Man, will suffer many things, be rejected by the Sanhedrin, and after three days be raised from the dead.

Luke 9:28-43a. The key to understanding Peter, John, and James's experience of Jesus' transfiguration lies in the fact that Jesus wants his intimate friends to know with clear certainty that, in spite of the terrible fate that awaits him, he is nonetheless the Messiah, the Chosen One, God's beloved Son.

After eight days, following Peter's recognition of Jesus as the Christ, Jesus goes with three disciples to a high mountain (probably Mount Tabor). Jesus goes up to pray. While praying, Jesus' countenance is changed ("transfigured"), and his clothes become dazzling white ("as bright as a flash of lightning").

Luke tells us that two men are talking with Jesus, Moses and Elijah. They discuss with Jesus his departure (death) that will take place in Jerusalem. While talking, Peter, John, and James (who are half-awake) realize what is happening. They see Jesus' glory and Moses and Elijah with him. Ask group members to discuss why Peter's suggestion that they build three shelters on the mountain upsets Jesus. How might they have known that Moses and Elijah were those revered forebears?

A voice, evoking a memory of the baptism of Jesus, comes out of the cloud and says, "This is my Son, whom I have chosen; listen to him." The two phrases carry many Old Testament memories and emotions. The cloud, as in Old Testament times, symbolizes the presence of God. (See Exodus 24:15-18; 1 Kings 8:10.)

Interestingly, after the voice of God speaks (for the benefit of Peter, John, and James?), they find themselves alone. They tell no one "at that time" what they have seen. (Why would the disciples tell no one of this great experience? Ask group members to venture guesses as to why.)

Luke 9:43b-50. Jesus tells his disciples a second time that "the Son of Man is going to be delivered into the hands of men." The repetition probably means the disciples did not understand or believe it. Jesus uses strong words: "Listen carefully." And Jesus might have added that these words should sink into your minds or you will not understand my future and your relationship to it.

Ask participants to share their thoughts on the following: In what way would prayer for understanding of Jesus' interpretation of his messianic ministry help us mature in faith? Not to pray for continuing insights into the life and message of Jesus is to exclude our chances of an "at-one-ment" with the mind of Christ or of being transformed by his Spirit. The disciples could not vibrate with the inner life of Jesus until after Jesus' resurrection and the Pentecost experience. We cannot reach the top of the ladder until we have first climbed up each rung.

The disciples, perhaps with some jealousy, see a man casting out demons in the name of Jesus. He is not a follower of Christ, so the disciples forbid him to do so. Jesus says, "Whoever is not against you is for you." Suggest a brief discussion of denominationalism from this perspective.

DIMENSION THREE: WHAT DOES THE BIBLE MEAN TO ME?

The group may discuss the following topic or questions, the suggested questions in this teaching plan, or use the material in the participant book.

Feeding the Multitudes

Some explanations (especially in sermons) indicate that the miracle in the feeding of the five thousand was that those who had brought along a little food were so moved by Jesus' words that they gave generously to extend the meal, allowing everyone to eat. If extravagant generosity is expected of all who love and follow Jesus, is it a miracle when people give? Think about current or recent humanitarian crises around the world: the growing numbers and increasing desperation in refugee camps; the thousands upon thousands of people displaced by natural disasters, such as hurricanes, and fires; the millions of citizens being repressed by the people or groups that control their lives. What kind of worldwide miracle would be required to address these problems and dangers? Is it even possible? Why or why not? Does your generosity of "sharing your little bit of lunch" make any difference? If so, how? If you think not, why do you give? If you're thinking about stopping, what might you first consider?

Luke 9:9—Who Is This Man?

Luke 9 deals with Herod's question "Who, then, is this I hear such things about?" Today's Scripture suggests several responses, chief of which is that of Peter ("God's Messiah"). We would do well to ask ourselves Herod's question.

What does it really mean to be a follower of Jesus Christ? As Peter stated, it means to believe that Jesus is truly the long-awaited Messiah. It also means to know Jesus' mind (by way of parables, similes, and metaphors). We are so to love his lifestyle that we enjoy a wonderful "at-one-ment" with him and with his purposes. We are quick and alert to respond to all opportunities to participate in the kingdom of God.

A danger exists in our claims to know and to be dedicated to the person of Jesus. We may develop a pride in our achievements. This attitude is exemplified in the foolish dispute of the disciples (9:46-48) as to which one of them would (or, more probably, should) be the greatest. Perhaps they all seek positions that will make them closest to the "power of the throne." It is a selfish and inexcusable attitude. Jesus deals with it by taking a child, apparently in his arms as Mark 9:36 suggests. Jesus' point is not that a leader needs a childlike character to enter the kingdom of God but rather that to accept Jesus himself, a leader must be prepared to accept and honor even those persons of our society who are lowliest in mental alacrity and spiritual achievements. Jesus wants the disciples to see that he respects and associates himself with the smallest and least. Jesus never feels honored above others because he dines with the most educated or most intelligent person present. He loves all and yearns for his followers to love all in the same way.

Follow me (9:59a).

6

JESUS SETS HIS FACE TOWARD JERUSALEM

Luke 9:51–11:28

DIMENSION ONE:
WHAT DOES THE BIBLE SAY?

Answer these questions by reading Luke 9:51-62

1. To what city does Jesus "resolutely set out"? (9:51)

   Jesus sets out for Jerusalem.

2. Before going to a Samaritan village, what does Jesus do? (9:52)

   Jesus sends messengers ahead of him.

3. How does Jesus respond to James and John, who want to destroy the Samaritans who refuse to receive him? (9:55-56)

   Jesus rebukes them; they go on to another village.

4. When a man says, "I will follow you wherever you go" (9:57), what is Jesus' response? (9:58)

   Jesus responds, "Foxes have dens and birds have nests, but the Son of Man has no place to lay his head."

5. Another man says, "Lord, first let me go and bury my father" (9:59). What is Jesus' response? (9:60)

   Jesus responds, "Let the dead bury their own dead, but you go and proclaim the kingdom of God."

6. A third man says, "First let me go back and say good-bye to my family" (9:61). What is Jesus' response? (9:62)

   Jesus responds, "No one who puts a hand to the plow and looks back is fit for service in the kingdom of God."

Answer these questions by reading Luke 10

7. How many followers does Jesus appoint to send into every town and place? (10:1)

   Jesus appoints seventy-two followers.

8. If a town does not receive them, what are they to say? (10:11)

   They are to say, "Even the dust of your town we wipe from our feet as a warning to you. Yet be sure of this: The kingdom of God has come near."

9. What reports do the seventy-two make to Jesus? (10:17)

   The seventy-two return with joy, saying, "Lord, even the demons submit to us in your name."

10. What is Jesus' response to their joyful reports? (10:18)

    Jesus replies, "I saw Satan fall like lightning from heaven."

11. In Jesus' prayer, for what does he praise God? (10:21)

    He thanks God for having "hidden these things from the wise . . . and revealed them to little children."

12. How are Jesus' disciples blessed? (10:23-24)

    They are blessed with both sensitive eyes and ears.

13. What question prompts the telling of the parable of the good Samaritan? (10:25)

    An expert in the law asks, "Teacher, . . . what must I do to inherit eternal life?"

14. Who is "my neighbor"? (10:29, 36-37)

"My neighbor" is the person who is merciful in one's time of need.

15. Who receives Jesus into her house? (10:38)

Martha receives Jesus into her house.

16. How does Mary upset Martha? (10:39-40)

Mary sits at Jesus' feet listening to his teaching instead of helping Martha prepare the meal.

Answer these questions by reading Luke 11:1-13

17. What is Luke's version of the Lord's Prayer? (11:2-4)

Luke's version of the Lord's Prayer is, "Father, / hallowed be your name, / your kingdom come. / Give us each day our daily bread. / Forgive us our sins, / for we also forgive everyone who sins against us. / And lead us not into temptation."

18. Why does the friend help his neighbor? (11:5-8)

The friend helps his neighbor because of his neighbor's persistence.

19. In order to receive, what must one do? (11:10)

One must ask in order to receive.

Answer these questions by reading Luke 11:14-28

20. When Jesus casts out a demon from a man who was mute, many are amazed. What do others say? (11:15)

Other people say, "By Beelzebul, the prince of demons, he is driving out demons."

21. What is Jesus' response? (11:17-20)

First, Jesus points out that a divided kingdom falls (therefore, would Satan cast out himself?). And second, Jesus affirms that it is by "the finger of God" that he drives out demons.

22. What happens when an impure spirit leaves a person? (11:24-26)

    The impure spirit returns with seven other spirits more wicked than itself.

23. What reply does Jesus make to the woman who says, "Blessed is the mother who gave you birth and nursed you"? (11:27-28)

    Jesus replies, "Blessed rather are those who hear the word of God and obey it."

DIMENSION TWO: WHAT DOES THE BIBLE MEAN?

In this lesson we begin a study of Jesus' journey from Galilee to Jerusalem, by way of Samaria. Luke provides a narrative framework in the form of a journey toward Jerusalem. The large literary work of Luke 9:51–19:27 is called the Lukan Insertion (into Mark's Gospel), or Luke's special section.

The geographical area covered in this Lukan Insertion is not clearly defined by Luke. But Jesus' travels are between the borders of Galilee and Judea. One Bible scholar remarks, "Once Jesus sets out on this lengthy journey, he seems to be no longer en route." That is, the teachings are more important than where he says them; so we are not informed as to specific places. In fact, we know very little about his location.

The Lukan Insertion (or special section) is a wonderful collection of Jesus' teachings: parables, legal and wisdom sayings, proverbs, critiques of sayings of his opponents, pronouncement teachings, and many miracle stories.

The Scripture is divided into five themes:

1. Conditions of Discipleship (9:51-62)
2. Mission of the Seventy-two (10:1-24)
3. Jesus Answers Questions (10:25-42)
4. Teachings About Prayer (11:1-13)
5. Casting Out Demons (11:14-26)

Luke 9:51-62. This section deals with Jesus' attitude toward Samaritans and people's readiness to follow Jesus. Jesus intentionally moves toward the place of religious authority, Jerusalem. "As the time approached for him to be taken up to heaven" (9:51) refers to Jesus' awareness of what lies in store for him. He knows the treatment that the prophets received at the hands of the people. Jesus goes to Jerusalem to make his last appeal to the religious leaders of Israel.

Jesus sends messengers (from among his disciples) to visit various villages to prepare for his coming. Two messengers soon report rejection by Samaritans when the Samaritans learn that Jesus is on his way to Jerusalem. Samaria was a capital city in the Northern Kingdom of Israel until it was conquered by the Assyrians in 721 BC. Jews who had not been taken into exile were left there, intermingling and eventually intermarrying with other subjects of the Assyrian Empire. Now, several centuries later, the Samaritans, who had ancient religious and cultural roots in Judaism, were considered as nothing better than impure mongrels by "real" Jews. The Samaritans' temple on Mount Gerizim was destroyed by the Jewish leader John Hyrcanus about 128 BC. The Samaritans still worshiped on Mount Gerizim and had their own festivals (the Festival of the Passover, Yom Kippur) and sacred Scripture (the Torah). Jews forbade Samaritans the right to worship in Jerusalem, but the Samaritans welcomed Jews at Mount Gerizim. Why should Jesus want to go to a temple built by the house of Herod? Why not worship at Gerizim?

James and John are angry at the Samaritans' apparent stubbornness and want to be rid of their kind. "Lord, do you want us to call fire down from heaven to destroy them?" The young men remember the story of a former prophet, Elijah, who said, "If I am a man of God, . . . may fire come down from heaven and consume you and your fifty men!" (2 Kings 1:12); and it did. How little these young fishermen understand Jesus' concept of the kingdom of God. The Kingdom is not to be coerced, nor is a curse put on those who reject God's call. Do the Samaritans not receive God's judgment? Yes, but they receive the kind of judgment that follows refusal of the good, the true, the attitudes and motives of the Lord God.

Ask group members to discuss Abraham Lincoln's response to the man who asked him why he was courteous to his enemies. Lincoln replied, "Do I not destroy my enemies when I make them my friends?" Similarly, Jesus turns and corrects his disciples. Then they go on to another village.

Luke 9:57-62 gives insight into Jesus' view of the nature of discipleship. Knowing his days are numbered, he welcomes those who want to become his followers. As they travel, several persons express interest in becoming his followers. One says, "I will follow you wherever you go." Jesus says to the aspirant, "Foxes have dens and birds have nests, but the Son of Man has no place to lay his head." Jesus is on his way to Jerusalem to die. His only home is God's home. The aspirant to discipleship is warned to count the cost. Ask participants: What is Jesus trying to communicate?

As they walk, Jesus invites another aspirant to join him. The aspirant replies, "Lord, first let me go and bury my father." Jesus values filial ties. However, the man's presence implies that his father may be getting old but is not yet dead. The young man could easily lose many months between his initial commitment and his actual following. Jesus needs persons who can decide and act for the Kingdom now. Jesus tells the man to let the spiritually dead bury the physically dead.

A third person says, "I will follow you, Lord; but first let me go back and say good-bye to my family." The price of discipleship includes being free of distractions, even loving ones. Looking back longingly and remembering fondly keeps our thoughts on the past. Jesus warns us to count the cost and to reckon with the conflict of loyalties that discipleship inevitably brings. Jesus probably remembers the story of Elijah seeking Elisha that he might put his prophetic cloak over his shoulders. Elijah found Elisha plowing with twelve yoke of oxen. He stopped Elisha in his work and placed his mantle over his shoulders. Elisha understood the symbol and begged Elijah to let him go home to kiss his father and mother good-bye. Elijah permitted it. (See 1 Kings 19:19-20.) But Jesus demands undivided loyalty.

Luke 10:1-24. The sending out of the seventy-two (or seventy in the NRSV) is recorded by Luke alone. Why does Jesus choose this number? Perhaps because the Hebrew text of Genesis 10 lists seventy Gentile nations and the Greek translation sometimes lists seventy-two. Eventually, they will teach all nations.

The return of the seventy-two is a joyful occasion. While Jesus notes how he "saw Satan fall like lightning from heaven," the disciples proudly tell how they worked miracles in Jesus' name. "Even the demons submit to us in your name," they say. But Jesus says, "Do not rejoice that the spirits submit to you, but rejoice that your names are written in heaven."

Jesus pauses with the seventy-two and prays to God, thanking God for revealing hidden things to these persons. Jesus says to his rejoicing disciples, "Blessed are the eyes that see what you see." Many persons see only the obvious physical things around them. But the spiritually minded see where God has left identifying marks of God's presence.

How great it is to be with friends whose vision is not limited to only what the physical eyes see. And how exciting to talk with those who "see" the kingdom of God, which many hear about but never see.

Luke 10:25-37. An expert in the law asks Jesus a question to test Jesus' moral and spiritual fiber: "What must I do to inherit eternal life?" That is, what must I do to know I have salvation? Jesus asks the lawyer, "What is written in the Law [the Torah]?" The lawyer responds by uniting verses from Deuteronomy 6:5 and Leviticus 19:18: "'Love the Lord your God with all your heart and with all your soul and with all your strength and with all your mind'; and, 'Love your neighbor as yourself.'" And Jesus says, "You have answered correctly. . . . Do this and you will live [be saved]."

Then the lawyer asks, "Who is my neighbor?" Jesus, instead of quoting outstanding rabbis or getting into a theological debate, tells a parable. As you read the parable, remember that for the Jew, a Samaritan is a half-breed descendant of the Israelites.

Read Luke 10:25-37 to the class and then discuss it. Notice the lawyer's significant question, "Who is my neighbor?" To answer this question, one must also know the answer to the question, Who is not my neighbor? Whom do we help and why? Where do we draw the line? Jews assumed that only Jews were their neighbors.

Second Chronicles 28:1-16 records a harrowing story with a more positive ending. As background, tell the class that King Pekah of Israel (Samaria) and King Rezin of Syria have been trying to force King Ahaz (of Jerusalem, Judah) into an alliance in order to stop the Assyrian forces from invading their lands. The two kings (of Samaria and Syria) invade Judah, leaving the people destitute.

Our concern focuses on Samaritan King Pekah whose armies slew one hundred twenty thousand Judean soldiers and took two hundred thousand captives. The Chronicler assumes a blood relationship between Samaritan and Jew; he states that the Samaritans "took captive from their fellow Israelites who were from Judah two hundred thousand wives, sons and daughters. They also took a great deal of plunder, which they carried back to Samaria" (28:8). Try to help group members visualize the terrible treatment the captives have received. They are naked, cold, abused, sick, weak, humiliated, beaten, and crippled.

Oded, a prophet, goes out to meet the victorious army and expresses strong opposition to their plans of enslaving their kinsfolk. "Aren't you also guilty of sins against the LORD your God?" he asks. "Now listen to me! Send back your fellow Israelites you have taken as prisoners." Four Samaritan chiefs stand up and support Oded against those who are coming from the war and say, "You must not bring those prisoners here." So the soldiers leave the captives and the spoil before the princes and all the assembly. The four chiefs "took the prisoners, and from the plunder they clothed all who were naked. They provided them with clothes and sandals, food and drink, and healing balm. All those who were weak they put on donkeys. So they took them back to their fellow Israelites at Jericho, the City of Palms, and returned to Samaria" (2 Chronicles 28:15). We might entitle this story *The Four Good Samaritans*.

Jesus' story involves a priest and a Levite, who are responsible for teaching and living the Torah. Their callousness stands in sharp contrast to the ideals over which they are the instructors and official guardians. They know the law but do not practice it.

In the story, the victim of a robber lies prostrate; three men come by. One is an ordinary priest who is on his way to Jerusalem to serve his required time in the temple. He knows he will be ritually unclean if he touches a dead man. The victim is "half dead." After all, leadership in religious ceremonies and rituals is important! The second person, a Levite (who also serves in turn in the temple), sees the victim; and thinking of his important status that he must protect, he walks by on the other side. Then comes the Samaritan, who ministers to the victim. Jesus asks the Jewish lawyer which of these men really loved his neighbor, as God commanded. "The one who had mercy on him" is the reply. Jesus says, "Go and do likewise." The conversation between Jesus and the teacher of the law illustrates the difference between the ethics of law and the ethics of love.

Luke 10:38-42. Luke probably purposely places the story of Mary and Martha in its present location. The good Samaritan was a doer of the word. In contrast, this story tells of the importance of faith attitudes. Martha has invited Jesus into her house. While she busily prepares a big meal—Is that not what would please Jesus?—Mary sits at his feet intently listening.

Martha's mind is filled with ideas for food to please the Master—lentils, crushed peas, roast lamb with mint jelly, olives. Mary's mind is filled with Jesus' concerns—his ministry and mission.

Martha is getting tense because she needs help with the meal, and perhaps she is a bit jealous of the exclusive attention Mary is receiving from Jesus. She asks Jesus to instruct Mary to join her in her busy task of preparing the meal. But Jesus does just the opposite, though in a kind way. He says in effect, "Martha, I have other needs just as important as a good meal. Mary has chosen the good portion. I am grateful to both of you." How else might the situation have been handled? Encourage group members to make other suggestions.

"To sit at the feet" of a person is to be his or her student, or disciple. In Acts 22:3, Paul says he was trained under his teacher Gamaliel. Mary is learning of the kingdom of God. Mary chooses the good portion.

Luke 11:1-4. In Luke's Gospel, the Lord's Prayer is shorter than in Matthew (6:9-13) but probably is closer to Jesus' original prayer. It is a challenging and inspiring prayer. It is difficult to pray the Lord's Prayer honestly. It presupposes a desire to be Christlike in our attitudes, motives, and dispositions. It presupposes our desire to experience God and to know God's will for our individual and corporate lives. If we do not share that desire, we really cannot pray as Jesus did or as he taught.

When speaking to one's father, the Jew would say *Abba* and to God *Abi*. Jews felt one should not address God with the same word used to address one's parent—it was too familiar and intimate. So Jesus breaks the custom. When he prays, he says *Abba* (translated "Father"), which includes the emotional overtones of respect, affection, and love. Jesus teaches his disciples to do the same.

To hallow God's name is done supremely by so living and speaking that your style reminds others of the Christlike God. Jesus hallowed God's name in his living. The kingdom of God is above all else. As we participate in the kingdom of God, we help fulfill the prayer "Your kingdom come." To permit hate, greed, jealousy, dishonesty, and unbridled passion to govern our lives denies our belief in and support of the kingdom of God.

The request "Give us each day our daily bread" implies that we are asking God to give us nourishment continually. Prayer includes the necessities of everyday life.

Ecclesiasticus (or Sirach) 28:2 explains the next petition about forgiveness of sins: "Forgive your neighbor the wrong he has done, / and then your sins will be pardoned when you pray." Jewish prayers insisted on the offender seeking forgiveness. Jesus insists that the injured person offer forgiveness. (Thus God can forgive.)

"Lead us not into temptation" presupposes the disciples' life in the world. They must learn to live in the context of the anxieties of the earthly life, and also they must learn to implore God for protection against the powerful attacks and temptations of the Evil One.

Luke 11:14-20. Jesus casts out a demon from a man who is mute without declaring that he is doing so in the name of God. For not saying by whose power he has exorcised the "demon" of muteness, some say, "By Beelzebul, the prince of demons, he is driving out demons." *Beelzebul* was the name of the Philistine god of Ekron, whose name was mockingly distorted by the Jews in the times of Elijah (see 2 Kings 1:2-3) to Baal-Zebub, which means "lord of the flies" as a corrupted form of "lord of the house." The Jews of Jesus' day know this distinction and are engaged in theological wordplay when they say Jesus has healed through the power of Beelzebul, "the prince of demons." They are thinking of their "fathers" when they use the name *Beelzebul*, which in Aramaic means "lord of dung."

Jesus equates Beelzebul with Satan and says that Satan cannot maintain power and authority if he willfully destroys the things he stands for—such as demons. On the other hand, Jesus is healing to set persons free. The finger of God has left the divine marks of God's presence in the exorcism Jesus performs. The two kingdoms confront each other in a war.

DIMENSION THREE:
WHAT DOES THE BIBLE MEAN TO ME?

The group may discuss the following topic or use the material in the participant book.

Jesus' Work and the Disciples' Work

Throughout these sessions, we see that Jesus spent a lot of time interacting with people in need, healing them, teaching them, directing them to the path of righteousness one way or another. Then, as a sort of advance crew for his intended visits, Jesus sent out his disciples to do the same work in his name. (Note Jesus' promise in John 14:12 and 14: "whoever believes in me will do the works I have been doing, and they will do even greater things than these, because I am going to the Father. . . . You may ask me for anything in my name, and I will do it.") And they did. Do you think that disciples today can heal others in the name of Christ as the original disciples did? Why or why not? When you think about all the works of Jesus, how can disciples today do "greater things than these"?

Jesus and Prayer

Invite group members to go through the Lord's Prayer line by line (either in Luke 11 or in the longer version in Matthew 6). Most of this know this so well by heart that reciting it may be just a rote exercise. Discuss the meaning and depth of each of the phrases. How well do you do day-to-day regarding living as if God is hallowed? as if you truly wish for the Kingdom to come? in forgiving others as you are forgiven?

Exorcism

The question of exorcism sometimes arises in our minds. How shall we understand and use it?

In postexilic and New Testament times, persons associated demons with disease and disabilities: blindness (Matthew 12:22), deafness (Mark 9:25), disorientation (Luke 8:30), epilepsy (Luke 9:39), and muteness (Luke 11:14).

Persons thought that demons lived in desert areas and that they were restless until they found their rest in human beings. To be free from demons, one participated in the annual exorcism of sin on the Day of Atonement. Leviticus 16:8-9, 20-22 describes actions of the chief priest, who chooses a goat at the same time he prepares a bull to sacrifice for the sins of all Jews. The priest puts his hands on the head of the goat, thereby transferring the sins of his people to the goat. When that is done, the goat is driven into the wilderness. Thus the goat is called the scapegoat because the peoples' sins have escaped them and have been put on an innocent sin-bearer, the goat. Though we do not offer scapegoats in our day, we practice the theory of it. How often is an innocent being (person) sacrificed to cover our own sin?

We exorcise demons of hate, greed, jealousy, irrational passions, dishonesty, and hypocrisy by sincerely repenting and seeking forgiveness of our sins. God absolves our sins by God's grace. Persons can be and are changed. We need to exorcise our own selves from demonic motives and thoughts. We do this by requesting power from the risen Lord, Jesus Christ. And that power is given and will be given.

You also must be ready, because the Son of Man will come at an hour when you do not expect him (12:40).

7
TRUE DISCIPLESHIP AND ITS OPPONENTS

Luke 11:29–13:9

DIMENSION ONE:
WHAT DOES THE BIBLE SAY?

Answer these questions by reading Luke 11:29-36

1. What sign will this generation receive? (11:29)

    This generation will receive "the sign of Jonah."

2. Jesus says that he embodies something greater than the talents of two great biblical persons. Who are they, and what are their talents? (11:31-32)

    Jesus says he embodies that which is greater than the wisdom of Solomon and the preaching of Jonah.

3. After lighting a lamp, where does one put it, and why? (11:33)

    After lighting a lamp, one places it on a stand "so that those who come in may see the light."

4. What serves to light the body, and how does it function? (11:34)

    The eye is the lamp of the body; and if the eye is healthy, the whole body is full of light.

Answer these questions by reading Luke 11:37–12:1

5. When Jesus dines with a Pharisee, what astonishes the Pharisee? (11:37-38)

    The Pharisee is surprised that Jesus does not wash before dinner.

6. What name does Jesus call the Pharisees? (11:40)
    Jesus calls the Pharisees foolish people.

7. What does Jesus condemn in his three "woes" to the Pharisees? (11:42-44)
    The Pharisees neglect justice and the love of God, they love the most important seats in the synagogues and greetings in the marketplaces, and they are like unmarked graves.

8. What does Jesus condemn in his three "woes" to the experts in the law? (11:46-47, 52)
    The experts in the law load persons "with burdens they can hardly carry," they build tombs for prophets that their ancestors killed, and they "have taken away the key to knowledge."

9. What does Jesus first say to the thousands who gather to hear him? (12:1)
    Jesus says, "Be on your guard against the yeast of the Pharisees, which is hypocrisy."

Answer these questions by reading Luke 12:2-48
10. What does Jesus say to those followers who may and will face persecution? (12:4)
    Jesus says, "My friends, do not be afraid of those who kill the body. . . . Fear him who, after your body has been killed, has authority to throw you into hell."

11. What is the unforgivable sin? (12:10)
    "Anyone who blasphemes against the Holy Spirit will not be forgiven."

12. What is more important than food and clothing? (12:23)
    Life is more important than food, and the body is more important than clothing.

13. Why is it important that one invest in "a treasure in heaven that will never fail"? (12:33-34)
    "Where your treasure is, there your heart will be also."

14. In what condition does the master expect to find his servants? (12:36-37a)
    The master expects to find his servants watching (alert).

15. What will the master do when he comes home? (12:37b)

    He will dress himself and serve them as they recline at the table.

16. What is the key to the demands the master places upon his various servants? (12:48b)

    "From everyone who has been given much, much will be demanded; and from the one who has been entrusted with much, much more will be asked."

Answer these questions by reading Luke 12:49–13:9

17. According to Jesus, does he come to bring peace or division? (12:51)

    Jesus comes to bring division.

18. How will a family experience this division? (12:53)

    A family will be divided, "father against son and son against father, mother against daughter and daughter against mother, mother-in-law against daughter-in-law and daughter-in-law against mother-in-law."

19. Why should persons attempt to settle their differences out of court? (12:57-58)

    Persons should learn to judge for themselves what is right and try hard to be reconciled.

20. What question does Jesus ask in order to turn a political issue (Pilate's slaying of several Galileans in the temple) into a religious issue? (13:2)

    Jesus asks, "Do you think that these Galileans were worse sinners than all the other Galileans because they suffered this way?"

21. What is Jesus' response to this religious issue? (13:3)

    Jesus says, "Unless you repent, you too will all perish."

22. What advice does the man give who took care of the vineyard give to the owner about the fruitless fig tree? (13:8-9)

    Leave it alone for a year; I'll dig around it and fertilize it. Then, if it bears no fruit, cut it down.

DIMENSION TWO:
WHAT DOES THE BIBLE MEAN?

The Scripture is divided into four themes:

1. The Sign of Jonah and Two Parables (11:29-36)
2. Denunciation of Pharisees and Lawyers (11:37–12:1)
3. Responsibilities of Discipleship (12:2-48)
4. Reflections on Christ's Ministry (12:49–13:9)

Luke 11:29-36. Jesus discusses the people's need for a sign immediately after he heals a man who was mute. Jesus has demonstrated his power and authority over the demonic. What he does for people, he does in the power of God. The kingdom of God is in their midst. He is the king of that kingdom. Why can they not see this truth?

Yet, miracles do not prove who Jesus is. People should not be expected to conclude that a temple-jumping stunt person is the Messiah. Jesus is more than a miracle worker. His message is the most important part of his ministry.

The apostle Paul writes, "Jews demand signs and Greeks look for wisdom, but we preach Christ crucified: a stumbling block to Jews and foolishness to Gentiles" (1 Corinthians 1:22-23). Signs, signs, signs! How Luke must have valued Jesus' statement that "this is a wicked generation. It asks for a sign, but none will be given it except the sign of Jonah" (Luke 11:29). Jonah was a living sign of God's authority, proclaiming the judgment of God to the people of Nineveh. So Jesus, in his life, preaching, and deeds, is the supreme sign of God's presence and action. Through Jesus, something greater than the wisdom of Solomon and greater than the preaching of Jonah has come. Jesus himself is the wisdom of the Greeks and the sign of the Jews.

John would declare that Jesus is the light of the world. As such, this "lamp" of God sheds light on those dwelling in the darkness of emptiness, hopelessness, and despair. This lamp is not covered; it is placed on a stand where the light is seen by all. Some Old Testament passages that probably aided Jesus in his understanding of himself as the light might be these: "You, LORD, keep my lamp burning; / my God turns my darkness into light" (Psalm 18:28); "For with you [God] is the fountain of life; / in your light we see light" (Psalms 36:9); "Here is my servant, whom I uphold. . . . / I will keep you and will make you / to be a covenant for the people / and a light for the Gentiles" (Isaiah 42:1, 6). You might ask three persons to look up these passages and read them aloud to the group.

Now read Luke 11:34-35 to participants. Ask them to discuss its meaning. Since the eye is the "lamp" of the body, what does that suggest both for what we let ourselves see and for what can be seen through us? Do we have an eye for spiritual things? Do we entertain thoughts that make for darkness of the soul and body? How do we keep the eye sound, so that our bodies are full of light?

The apostle Paul introduced the word *conscience* to our Christian vocabulary. A person who has no conscience is spiritually blind. He or she misses some things in life, unable to see the light of the lamp of God.

Luke 11:37–12:1. Group members may have an interest in knowing who the Pharisees and teachers of the law (scribes, lawyers) are—and how they differ. History does not supply us with the means of determining the precise period when the Pharisees and scribes appeared as religious groups. The religious emphases of both groups go back to the period of exile in Babylon (from 586 BC to 538 BC). Denied the use of the temple, the rites and festivals were "memorialized"; that is, they were remembered but were not literally carried out. The exiles replaced the temple with synagogues, which served as places of instruction in the Scriptures and prayer. Emphasis was placed on obedience to the laws of Moses and eventually to an elaborate system of oral tradition.

About 458 BC, a number of Jews from Babylon returned to Judea, bringing with them the books of the Torah. After Ezra read the Torah (the first five books of the Bible) to the Judeans, it was adopted as the law and became the foundation of Judaism. The sacrificial system was restored with its powerful priests, who were still responsible for instruction in the law as well as oversight of temple duties. But a new group of lay lawyers, called scribes, came into being. The scribes were not necessarily priests; they served more in the capacity of assistants.

Now the law, not the temple, became the primary factor in Judaism (postexilic Jewish life). The scribes, the interpreters of the law, now became free to oppose the temple. These lay scribes, lawyers trained in interpretation and application of the law, now became the religious leaders of Judaism.

The scribes formed the core of the group called Pharisees. The scribes were the learned members. The word *Pharisee* means "separated," a nickname for those who, in their meticulous observance of the law, "separated themselves" from the ritually unclean.

To assure ritual cleanliness, the scribes developed hundreds of oral laws that were applications made on the various Mosaic laws. These interpretations and applications are called "the traditions of the elders." The intent of the elders was good. Eventually, however, the oral (unwritten) traditions of the elders became more important than the original Mosaic law and the ethical claims of the prophets. The Pharisees and the scribes believed in immortality, with rewards or punishments according to the way a person has lived in this life. They also believed in resurrection. Politically, they were very powerful. They became the real administrators of public affairs. Jesus emphasizes this point in his parables.

While Jesus is teaching, a Pharisee invites Jesus to dine with him. Jesus accepts the invitation. When they sit down at the table, the Pharisee observes that Jesus has not washed his hands and therefore does not uphold one of the traditions of the elders. The question is not one of hygiene but one of ritual.

What does this ritual washing before dinner involve? One day, while eating lunch in a restaurant in New York City, I witnessed a man "washing his hands" as he sat at his table before he ate lunch. He rolled up his sleeves to his elbows; held his hands slightly above the table top; and poured a small quantity of water over the tips of his fingers, letting the water run to his wrist. Then he cleaned the palm of each hand by rubbing the fist of the other into it. Lastly, he poured the remaining water over his hands, beginning with his wrist and running down to the fingertips. I sympathized with what I at first thought was eccentricity until I suddenly realized what was taking place. He was a Hasidic Jew who was fulfilling one of the traditions of the elders by being ritually clean before eating.

The unwritten (oral) law requires a pious Jew to use at least a quarter of a log (enough to fill one and one-half egg shells) of water for this ceremony. The ritual is to be done in the order prescribed (noted in my illustration). To omit the slightest detail is to commit sin.

Jesus comments to his host, who has "noticed that Jesus did not first wash before the meal," "You Pharisees clean the outside of the cup and dish, but inside you are full of greed and wickedness. You foolish people! Did not the one who made the outside make the inside also?" (11:39-40). Does not your inner life need cleansing too? Which is more important, to be clean within or without? You Pharisees are careful to give alms (coins) to the poor publicly, but you should learn to give gifts from within: Give hope, faith, love, and justice.

Jesus pronounces three woes to the Pharisees and three to the scribes. Ask group members to keep in mind that the scribes are the interpreters of the law; the Pharisees (with the exception of the scribal core) are those who are concerned with obedience to the law as interpreted.

"Woe to [in the sense of "Alas for"] you Pharisees," Jesus says, for your externalism, pride in legalistic religion, religious ostentation, and pious hypocrisy. We have already noted an example of externalism in their desire to wash their hands ceremoniously without cleansing their thoughts and attitudes. (See 11:37-40.) Jesus also rebuffs them for their legalistic religion. Jesus says, "You neglect justice and the love of God" (11:42).

Then Jesus adds the second woe: religious ostentation. Pharisees, in their pride of obeying all the laws the scribes could tally up, want recognition in their synagogues. They sit in the front seats. As they enter the synagogues, they are properly greeted and saluted by their peers and honored by persons of lesser qualifications in back of them. They are similarly welcomed when they go to the marketplaces and bask in the sunlight of their religiosity (11:43).

The third woe condemns the Pharisees for pious hypocrisy. Most persons assume the Pharisees are as impeccable in morality and conduct as they are in their practice of religion. Jesus thinks of Numbers 19:16, which states that if a person is walking in a field and unknowingly touches a dead body or walks over a grave, he or she is unclean and cannot worship for seven days. Many Pharisees, by their inner corruption, make those around them unclean by their contact with them. They are "like unmarked graves, which people walk over without knowing it" (11:44). They could be likened to moral lepers who ought to say, "I'm unclean. Don't come near me; my sins are contagious."

Jesus also gives three woes to the scribes. (See 11:45-54). Luke, thinking of his Gentile readers, does not use the word *scribes*—for that would be interpreted as persons who write letters and documents. Instead, Luke substitutes *experts in the law*. Jesus condemns the lawyers (scribes), first of all, for loading down the average person "with burdens they can hardly carry." Behind this phrase are the thousand-and-one ways of breaking the Ten Commandments, according to the oral traditions of the elders. For several hundred years the teachers of the law had interpreted each of the Ten Commandments in terms of applications and illustrations. For example, a person could break the commandment "Remember the Sabbath day by keeping it holy" (Exodus 20:8) in 613 different ways. The scribes' job was to unlock the Scriptures.

To carry a burden on the Sabbath is illegal, if you carry it in your usual manner. But if you carry it in an unusual manner, such as on the back of your hand; with your foot, your mouth, or your ear; or in your shoe, that is legal. Such petty interpretations of God's will infuriate Jesus. These interpretations portray God as unthinking and amoral in character. Also, the unwritten (oral) traditions become such a burden, the common people cannot do both their daily work and fulfill the (oral) laws of God. Jesus realizes these interpretations and applications of the Mosaic law are replacing the true law (the Torah).

Jesus also condemns the scribes who honor only the dead prophets (such as Amos, Hosea, Isaiah, Jeremiah) and have even built tombs honoring them. The scribes believe that God has spoken what God wants to speak in the law. They are not likely to listen to a new, living prophet. Their dedication to law makes the messages of the prophets secondary, whereas Jesus puts the prophets in first place. (See 11:47-48.) The present generation must break with the past by repentance.

Jesus hurls his third woe at the experts in the law for having "taken away the key to knowledge," burying it in all the rules of the oral traditions of the elders. Thus the scribes are not the teachers of the law but a hindrance to God and his people. Woe to them! Instead of being guardians of the law, they have built fences that keep believers away from God. They obscure rather than clarify God's purposes, God's covenant, God's kingdom.

Naturally the lawyers and the Pharisees do not like Jesus' evaluation of their practices. So they begin "to oppose him fiercely and to besiege him with questions, waiting to catch him in something he might say" (11:53-54). Little wonder that Jesus tells his disciples, "Be on your guard against the yeast of the Pharisees, which is hypocrisy" (12:1).

Luke 12:2-48. The rabbis' sermons were not logically developed as are those of most ministers of our time. The rabbis had several key points ("pearls of wisdom"), generally unrelated, that they wanted to make. We have several pearls in this section of the lesson.

One pearl assures the disciples not to be afraid of "those who kill the body." By implication, they are to fear the "yeast of the Pharisees" whose emphasis on obedience to oral laws stifles and eventually kills the soul. Therefore be loyal to Jesus' teachings, even if you must face martyrdom. Death cannot kill the spirit of the person whose body they killed. All persons die physically, but physical death does not have the last word. They should learn to "fear him [God] who, after your body has been killed, has authority to throw you into hell" (12:5). God does not forget. Loyal ones will continue in eternal life because God values them as persons.

Another pearl of the jewels of the spirit is to give undivided loyalty, not to scribal laws, but to the person of Jesus Christ. (See 12:8-12.) Every person either acknowledges or denies spiritual kinship with Jesus Christ. The person who refuses commits the unpardonable sin. The unpardonable sin is the deliberate refusal to accept God's truth as it is made known to us through Jesus. Ernest Fremont Tittle once wrote, "The 'sin against the Holy Spirit' is not, of course, some one particular sin; it is a human will set deliberately and persistently against truth and right and love. No one who . . . truly desires the forgiveness of God has 'blasphemed' against the Holy Spirit" (*The Gospel According to Luke*; Harper & Row, 1951; page 134).

The unforgivable sin is simply to say no to God and never change that response. This sin is unforgivable because forgiveness comes in response to repentance. Jesus' preaching for repentance is his call to admit our folly, our stupidity, our sinful intent, and to experience the divine forgiveness of our sins.

Jesus' parable of the rich fool (12:13-21) is told in response to a man who is unhappy with his inheritance settlement. Perhaps Jesus recalls the time when Moses saw two brother Hebrews struggling together and he asked the man who did the wrong, "Why are you hitting your fellow Hebrew?" (Exodus 2:13). The Hebrew answered, "Who made you ruler and judge over us?" (Exodus 2:14). Jesus, in a similar spirit, says to the younger brother, "Man, who appointed me a judge or an arbiter between you?"

Jesus sees the men as members of the same family, as worshipers in the same synagogue, readers of the same law and prophets. Jesus responds by telling a parable that might show the futility of covetousness. Ask a group member to read aloud Luke 12:13-21. After the reading, you might reread verse 15 ("Watch out! Be on your guard against all kinds of greed; life does not consist in an abundance of possessions.") and verse 20 ("You fool! This very night your life will be demanded from you. Then who will get what you have prepared for yourself?"). So a person who lays up treasures for himself or herself is often poverty-stricken toward God. Discuss this statement: Today the chief end of many persons is to gain lots of money, regardless of consequences. Contrast this "chief end" with Jesus' statement, "Sell your possessions and give to the poor. Provide purses for yourselves that will not wear out" (12:33).

Luke 12:49–13:9. Jesus says he came "to bring fire on the earth." He brings disturbance and division by the nature of his teachings and his demand for decision. His teachings contradict and nullify the oral traditions of the elders, as taught by Pharisees and scribes. So they kindle fires to destroy his ministry. Jesus changes all persons with the warmth of God's love. Many brothers, sisters, parents, and children dislike the new person that conversion brings, and division and bitterness result. Even Jesus' own family thinks he is out of his mind (Mark 3:21). Jesus has to ask, "Who are my mother and my brothers?" (Mark 3:33).

In Luke 13:1-9, Jesus deals with the political aspects of life. Pilate killed some Galileans while they were preparing their sacrifices. Many Jews are urging Jesus to speak a message of revolt. Jesus, however, raises several theological questions: Did God cause these sinners to die? Was sin the issue? Might their deaths have been avoided if they had been warned? Are you not in constant danger from God's judgment? You are in danger. Beware!

The closing parable tells about "a man [who] had a fig tree growing in his vineyard, and he went to look for fruit on it but did not find any." A vineyard in Palestine would contain both vines and fruit trees. The owner comes to the fig tree and finds no fruit; it has not been fruitful for three years. So he suggests cutting down the tree, for it is using up the nutrients of the good earth. The person who takes care of the vineyard recommends one more year with cultivation and fertilizer. If the tree produces no fruit next year, well and good, cut it down. The parable of the barren fig tree symbolizes the period of grace that the nation has been granted for repentance. So people are to be productive or repent and experience God's mercy for another try.

DIMENSION THREE:
WHAT DOES THE BIBLE MEAN TO ME?

The group may discuss this topic or use the material in the participant book.

"Pearls" of Insight

Luke preserves a beautiful "pearl" when he quotes Jesus' saying, "Provide purses for yourselves that will not wear out, a treasure in heaven that will never fail, where no thief comes near and no moth destroys" (12:33b). To become rich in God's sight, one must begin with a repentant plea: "I am poor in spirit, poverty-stricken in soul. Give me faith, hope, love, and empathy for those living in substandard conditions." We must ask, Are we rich toward God or rich in things?

We find a second "pearl" of great price in 11:34: "When your eyes are healthy, your whole body also is full of light." We may ask ourselves, *Do we have an eye for spiritual things?*

Second Kings 6:11-23 tells of the king of Aram who tried to capture and kill Elisha, but somehow Elisha seemed to anticipate the king's every military strategy. Elisha's servant awoke and realized the Aramean army completely encircled him and Elisha. He awakened his master and cried, "Oh no, my lord! What shall we do?" Elisha replied, "Don't be afraid. . . . Those who are with us are more than those who are with them." Elisha prayed, saying, "Open his eyes, LORD, so that he may see." And the young man could see that the mountains were full of horses and chariots of fire round about Elisha.

When the Arameans came toward them, Elisha prayed that they be struck blind; and he led the blinded army to Samaria. There he prayed, "LORD, open the eyes of these men so they can see." And the men could see the mess they were in. The king of Israel asked, "Shall I kill them?" Elisha responded, "Set food and water before them so that they may eat and drink and then go back to their master." So the king prepared a great feast for them; and when they had eaten and drunk, he sent them back to their master. "So the bands from Aram stopped raiding Israel's territory."

How attitudes determine what we can see! How is our spiritual sight? What do we see? What do we not see? What is the purpose of a parable? What should it mean to me? A parable calls for the hearer's participation and involvement. The involvement is not so much on the intellectual level as in the affective (emotional) domain. We are to "feel" for the lost, younger son and his father; for the rich man who never disciplined himself; for the widow who lost one of the few coins of her social security. Then suddenly we "feel" joy, exuberance, and boundless faith. In these varying moods our emotions listen to the good news Jesus brings. Then the mind understands the feelings; and we find wholeness, peace, and healing.

Woe Is Me!

Jesus heaped a load of criticism on the Pharisees and scribes. Form small groups of three or four participants and divide among them the woes for discussion. Ask what the woe means to the scribe or Pharisee and what examples are prevalent today. Encourage participants to "see the mote in their own eyes," even if they do not discuss it.

The woes:

- Showing outward signs of piety without changing the corruption within
- Showing undue ostentation in their religious practices (being "holier than thou")
- Being hypocritical in their personal piety
- Burdening the faithful with the jot and tittle of the religious rules
- Honoring only prophets who were dead and failing to recognize prophets in their midst
- Obscuring, rather than clarifying the law

Make every effort to enter through the narrow door, because many, I tell you, will try to enter and will not be able to (13:24).

THE LIFE OF DISCIPLESHIP

Luke 13:10–15:32

DIMENSION ONE:
WHAT DOES THE BIBLE SAY?

Answer these questions by reading Luke 13:10-35

1. Where is Jesus when he cures a woman? (13:10-13)

    Jesus is in a synagogue.

2. Why is the synagogue leader upset? (13:14)

    He is indignant because Jesus healed the woman on the Sabbath.

3. What does the synagogue leader say to the people? (13:14)

    He says, "There are six days for work. So come and be healed on those days, not on the Sabbath."

4. What does Jesus say to the synagogue leader? (13:15-16)

    He says, "Doesn't each of you on the Sabbath untie his ox or donkey from the stall and lead it out to give it water? Then should not this woman . . . be set free on the Sabbath day from what bound her?"

5. Jesus compares the kingdom of God with what two things? (13:18-21)

    He compares the kingdom of God to a mustard seed and to yeast.

6. When someone asks how many will be saved (13:23), what is Jesus' reply? (13:24-30)

   He answers that "Abraham, Isaac and Jacob and all the prophets [and] . . . people . . . from east and west and north and south . . . will take their places at the feast in the kingdom of God." But "many . . . will try to enter and will not be able to."

7. When some Pharisees tell Jesus he should "leave this place and go somewhere else" because Herod wants to kill him, what does Jesus say? (13:31-33)

   Jesus says that he will continue to follow his planned schedule.

8. After Jesus laments over Jerusalem, when does he hint he will be there? (13:35b)

   "I tell you, you will not see me again until you say, 'Blessed is he who comes in the name of the Lord!'"

Answer these questions by reading Luke 14

9. One Sabbath while dining with a "prominent Pharisee," what does Jesus do? (14:1-6)

   He heals a man who is suffering from abnormal swelling.

10. What is Jesus' main point in the parable on choosing a seat at the wedding feast? (14:11)

    "For all those who exalt themselves will be humbled, and those who humble themselves will be exalted."

11. Whom does Jesus recommend you invite to a feast? (14:12-13)

    Do not invite those who can invite you in return; invite persons who are poor, crippled, lame, and blind.

12. Why will you be blessed for inviting these people? (14:14)

    You will be blessed because they cannot repay you.

13. What excuses do people make who are invited to a great banquet? (14:18-20)

    One person says, "I have just bought a field, and I must go and see it." Another says, "I have just bought five yoke of oxen, and I'm on my way to try them out." A third person says, "I just got married, so I can't come."

14. In anger the master tells his servant to go out and get some guests. Whom does he say to get? (14:21-23)

> *He says to go out into the streets and alleys and "bring in the poor, the crippled, the blind and the lame." Then the servant is to go to the roads and country lanes and compel people to come in.*

15. What four challenges does Jesus give to those who want to be his disciples? (14:26-35)

> *1. You must learn to hate your father, mother, wife, child, brother, sister, even your own life.*
>
> *2. You must carry your own cross and follow him.*
>
> *3. You must count the cost.*
>
> *4. You must be "salty" persons.*

16. To whom does Jesus say, "Whoever has ears to hear, let them hear"? (14:25, 35)

> *Jesus makes this statement to the large crowds who are traveling with him.*

Answer these questions by reading Luke 15

17. What is the cause of the muttering of the Pharisees and the teachers of the law? (15:2)

> *The Pharisees and teachers of the law are muttering because Jesus welcomes tax collectors and sinners and eats with them.*

18. Where does the shepherd who loses a sheep leave his ninety-nine other sheep while searching for the lost one? (15:4)

> *He leaves them in the open country.*

19. As a woman and her friends will rejoice in her finding a lost silver coin, who will rejoice over one sinner who repents? (15:10)

> *"There is rejoicing in the presence of the angels of God over one sinner who repents."*

20. What is the major sign of the younger son's degradation? (15:15-16)

> *He becomes a herdsman for pigs, which are regarded as very unclean, and is so hungry he would gladly eat their food.*

21. What does the younger son think his relationship to his father is? (15:19)

    He plans to tell his father, "I am no longer worthy to be called your son; make me like one of your hired servants."

22. How does the father receive his lost son? (15:20b-24)

    The father sees, has compassion for, runs toward, embraces, and kisses his son. Then the father orders clothes, a ring, and sandals for his son and prepares a feast to celebrate the son's return.

23. How does the elder son react to the younger son's return? (15:25-30)

    The elder son becomes angry because he has served his father well all these years and never has his father given a banquet for him and his friends.

DIMENSION TWO: WHAT DOES THE BIBLE MEAN?

The Scripture for this lesson, "The Life of Discipleship," is divided into five themes:

1. Sabbath and God's New Creation (13:10-21)
2. Teachings During the Journey (13:22-35)
3. Table Talk in the House of a Pharisee (14:1-24)
4. The Conditions of Discipleship (14:25-35)
5. God's Love for the Lost (15:1-32)

Luke 13:10-21. Luke, a Gentile doctor, here tells of a woman who "was bent over and could not straighten up at all" (13:11). Luke is telling a story of God's healing of a Jewish woman who has suffered for eighteen years. And marvel of marvels, she is cured in a synagogue—an unheard-of place for a woman even to be seen, let alone recognized—called to come to the front of the synagogue and to receive healing. How excited Luke is as he records the beautiful story. It must have been difficult for him not to use adjectives as he describes Jesus placing his hands on the woman, who is then immediately restored to standing straight.

This scene takes place in a synagogue—Luke's last recorded appearance of Jesus in a synagogue. The significance of this miracle comes with the objection in 13:14, answered by two counter questions (verses 15-16). Luke felt that something deeper lay behind this miracle. In a way, the healing of this woman points to the new era. Try to imagine Jesus seeing her behind the latticework in the back of the synagogue. Her very presence cries out to him for healing, and he calls her to come forward—to the seats of the Pharisees in the front row. Jesus puts his hands on her, she is healed, and she praises God.

What about the synagogue leader? He does not praise God; he is indignant because Jesus has performed work on the Sabbath. One of the works forbidden on the Sabbath is to heal. You could put a bandage on a wound as long as you put no healing ointments on it. You could keep a sufferer from getting worse, but you were not allowed to better the person's condition. Jesus violates the law. The synagogue leader calls for quiet and states his authoritative position: "There are six days for work. So come and be healed on those days, not on the Sabbath."

Jesus knows that religious leaders take their ox and donkey to water on the Sabbath. He says, "You hypocrites! . . . Then should not this woman, a daughter of Abraham, whom Satan has kept bound for eighteen long years, be set free on the Sabbath day from what bound her?" (just as you loosen the bonds for the ox and the donkey on the Sabbath day). The people are delighted; the religious leaders are humiliated. This is the focus of the text.

After such a healing and rejoicing, Jesus asks, "What is the kingdom of God like?" (13:18-21). The Kingdom starts in small ways, as with a mustard seed that grows until it can offer nesting to birds of all kinds in its branches. Also, the Kingdom is like yeast or leaven that likewise begins in small measure but when put in dough soon rises and changes the nature and taste of the bread. The kingdom of God has small beginnings in the lives of persons, families, and nations; but its potential is great.

Luke 13:22-35. This passage focuses entirely on Jerusalem. On their way to Jerusalem, many persons ask Jesus questions. One person asks, "Lord, are only a few people going to be saved?" Who will be saved? Pharisees and teachers of the law but few others? By what are persons saved, and from what are they saved? Is a person saved by being a son or daughter of David—automatic salvation because of place and family of birth? (In our day we might ask, Are we saved by our genes and chromosomes?) What does it mean to be saved?

The oral tradition of law attempted to cover any situation that involved breaking the Mosaic law, and as such was focused on so much detail that the spirit of the law could be lost in the midst of it. Those attempting to follow hundreds of specific regulations sometimes kept a personal score card to ensure that they observed the law at least 51 percent of the time, thus, they believed, securing their salvation. Jesus challenged this score-keeping notion with a newer, broader reality of what was salvific and what was not. Paradoxically, this broader reality of the vastness of God's grace for humankind, is also a "narrow" way because it means following a hard path—not legalistic rules and regulations, but the grace-filled command to love all others and to serve God wholeheartedly. Though simple to describe, Jesus knew it would be difficult to do. We like our comfort and want to avoid risk or spiritual depth that may ask of us more than we are willing to commit to.

Jesus said, "Make every effort to enter through the narrow door, because many, I tell you, will try to enter and will not be able to" (13:24). Strive, not to be obedient to rules made by humankind, but to know and do the will of God. The prophets (such as Amos, Hosea, and Isaiah) struggled to know the will of God. They concluded, Act justly, love mercy, and walk humbly with your God (Micah 6:8). Striving to enter by the narrow door means agonizing over the will of God in prophetic stance until we identify with God's will as seen in the life and teachings of Jesus. Striving to enter by the narrow door means to know and strongly assert the will of God in all life. This striving is the meaning of, "Take up your cross."

Those who "enter through the narrow door" have agonized and sweated drops of blood, as it were, to know, accept, and assert God's will. Those who do not will hear the door close, seek to enter, and not be able to do so (13:24). Once outside, you knock and say, "Open to us. We ate church dinners in your presence, and you taught through your dedicated teachers in our classes and streets." But he will say, "I don't know you or where you come from."

What is the source of your faith? Is it the oral traditions of your admired ancestors? Is your faith a living well of water that quenches your thirst for the abundant life? Those who are workers of iniquity will weep and gnash their teeth—for you will "see Abraham, Isaac and Jacob and all the prophets in the kingdom of God, but you yourselves thrown out" (13:28). The meaning is getting all too clear, isn't it?

In Luke 13:31-33, Luke shares the news that not all Pharisees are against Jesus. Some Pharisees come to warn Jesus that Herod Antipas wants to kill him. Herod killed Jesus' kinsman, John (son of Zechariah and Elizabeth), and apparently considers Jesus to be a revolutionary who might lead a revolt against Rome. So Herod wants to see and to talk with Jesus. Jesus knows Herod is as cunning and scheming as a fox. Jesus asks these friendly Pharisees to get word to Herod that he has a full schedule and will not change it just to see a king. In a short time Jesus will be in Jerusalem, where he wants to make his last appeal to the religious leadership of Judah.

Jesus' lament over Jerusalem follows the challenging statements in 13:32-34. "How often I have longed" presupposes Jesus' having been in Jerusalem a number of times. He even weeps over Jerusalem because the people do not know the style of life that makes for peace.

Many times Jesus would have thought of Deuteronomy 32:11, "Like an eagle that stirs up its nest / and hovers over its young, / that spreads its wings to catch them / and carries them aloft" and of Psalm 36:7, "How priceless is your unfailing love, O God! / People take refuge in the shadow of your wings." Do you hear the cry of the Master, "Jerusalem, Jerusalem, you who kill the prophets and stone those sent to you, how often I have longed to gather your children together, as a hen gathers her chicks under her wings, and you were not willing. Look, your house is left to you desolate" (Luke 13:34-35a)?

In 13:35, we may have a suggested date of Jesus' appearance in Jerusalem, Palm Sunday. Jesus says he will not see Jerusalem until they say, "Blessed is he who comes in the name of the Lord." This verse is from Psalm 118:26, one of the six Hallel (praise the Lord) psalms sung at the Festival of the Passover. In Jesus' time the crowds observed Passover by singing the Hallel psalms and by waving the Hosanna palms. This occasion would be the great day of Jesus announcing publicly, for the first time, that he is the Messiah. Jerusalem would see him riding on a lowly donkey, the symbol of humility.

Luke 14:1-24. In Luke 14:1-6, we have Luke's account of Jesus' fourth healing on the Sabbath. The first time, Jesus healed a man of an impure spirit in the synagogue at Capernaum (Luke 4:31-36). The second time, he healed a man with a shriveled right hand (6:6-11). The third time, he healed the woman who had been bent over for eighteen years (13:10-17). The fourth time, as Jesus dines in the home of a Pharisee (14:1-6), he cures a man who has severe edema. (Luke records two other times that Jesus was in the homes of Pharisees: Luke 7:36-50, when a woman poured expensive perfume on his feet; and Luke 11:37-44, when Jesus condemned the Pharisees for obeying the oral traditions of the elders rather than obeying the prophets.)

In 14:1-6, Jesus is again in the home of a leader of the Pharisees, where some Pharisees are watching him carefully. They apparently have planted a person in their midst who has an "abnormal swelling," what was once called dropsy. *Dropsy* comes from the Greek word *hudropilos*, meaning "too much water." In English today the word used for this condition is *edema*. The old question comes up again, Can we support working on the Sabbath in the case of healing? Jesus heals the man of his edema, then asks the watching Pharisees, If you had a child or an ox that had fallen into a well, would you not immediately draw him out so that he would not drown? So if you have a man drowning in the water of his body (edema) on the Sabbath, should we not save his life? Jesus challenges his host, exposing him to God's new creation. God's Sabbath seeks to free the Pharisee, who bars the way to his suffering neighbor.

Perhaps Jesus is provoked that the Pharisees sought to prevent the healing of the man. In Greek, healing is also saving; and being saved is being healed. What better time to be healed/saved than when engaged in worship? Let the Sabbath be known as the time when God's healing/saving is offered to all.

In Luke 14:7-14, we read of Jesus' teaching on humility. The purpose of the parable is to suggest appropriate responses to the offer of the kingdom of God. In the parable a man of relatively high standing arrives early and chooses a nice seat near the host. As others come, they seat themselves "below" him; soon the places are all taken. Then a person with considerable prestige arrives and is invited to the head of the table, to the very seat held by the man who arrived early. Of course he is asked to give up his place to the man of honor—which, since all other seats are taken, puts him in the last seat. "All those who exalt themselves will be humbled, and those who humble themselves will be exalted." Jesus has no concern for status.

Jesus, in the second part of the parable, says, if you give a party, do not always invite just your relatives and your close friends—people you feel close to and with whom you have a spiritual kinship. But see the needs of people who are poor, who have disabilities, who are blind regarding spiritual fellowship and growth. They have no opportunity to rub shoulders with those who have great ideas and a life-giving faith. Feed these marginalized people with hope, faith, and charity. Some people sit at home, lonely and hungering for life. They look through their windows as the messianic feast is offered and wonder if there is bread for them too. The reward for feeding bread of life to persons on the fringe of "respectability" will be yours as you see them in the Resurrection.

Closely related to the above is the parable of the great banquet (Luke 14:15-24). When one of the guests sitting near Jesus hears Jesus' first parable, he (looking around at all the guests, who are Pharisees) piously says to Jesus, "Blessed is the one who will eat at the feast in the kingdom of God." The word *blessed* may well have meant "O the happiness of those, like us, who will eat bread in the Kingdom." Remembering their obedience to legal traditions rather than to prophetic teachings, Jesus tells another parable—about a great banquet. Through the parable Jesus raises the question of motives and our basic loyalties.

The guests are invited; and when the feast is ready, the host sends his servants to those invited, telling them it is time to come. But many of the guests make excuses. One is a business excuse, the man has just purchased a field and yearns to see it. Another person has just purchased five yoke of oxen and wants to examine his ox-power. Still another man states he has just married and therefore cannot go. (This excuse is legally valid; for the law in Deuteronomy 24:5 says, "If a man has recently married, he must not be sent to war or have any other duty laid on him. For one year he is to be free to stay at home and bring happiness to the wife he has married.")

The parable lists excuses persons use for not giving full allegiance to the kingdom of God. The Jews had been waiting for centuries for the day of the Lord. Now it has come through the person of Jesus. But the people refuse to come to the greatest of all feasts, the messianic banquet, where the host is Jesus of Nazareth. In the parable Jesus has the angry host ordering the servant to go to the city streets and alleys and invite "the poor, the crippled, the blind and the lame." To fill the still empty seats, the host then tells the servant to call Gentiles to come (14:23). None of those who were invited first (the Pharisees and experts in the law) shall taste the banquet. The invitation goes far beyond all expectations. Those who were invited first have done nothing wrong; they have just failed to respond to the invitation.

Luke 14:25-35. Keep in mind the setting: Jesus is going through Samaria to Jerusalem and is facing possible crucifixion. He is paying a great price for accepting messiahship. What conditions might would-be followers expect to assume? Jesus tells of four conditions, which you might write on a whiteboard, a chalkboard, or a large piece of paper: (1) Have no greater love than love for Christ. (2) Carry your own cross. (3) Count the cost of your commitment. (4) Be "salty" persons.

In the first condition for discipleship we find a difficult statement: "If anyone comes to me and does not hate father and mother, wife and children . . ." (14:26). Jesus uses a Semitic hyperbole ("hate") to exaggerate a contrast to make the difference obvious. Luke, writing in Greek, uses the term *miseo*, meaning "loves less than." This idiom is illustrated in Genesis 29:30-31. Read the entire account in Genesis 29:21-31 to group members. Jacob fell in love with Rachel and thought he had married her—only to discover that Laban (his father-in-law) had substituted Leah, the older daughter. Jacob agrees to work seven years to "earn" Rachel, for "his love for Rachel was greater than his love for Leah." Genesis 29:31 restates Jacob's love for Rachel by saying, in idiomatic form in Hebrew, "Leah was hated"; that is, Jacob loved Leah less than he loved Rachel.

So Jesus uses an exaggeration that all persons in his day understood but which, when taken literally, obliterates the intended meaning. Jesus is saying that primary allegiance must be made to God. You are expected to love God more than you love your family. If you cannot do this, do not ask to be a follower of Christ.

The second point Jesus makes is to carry your own cross, which means doing what you think God wants you to do regardless of the consequences. Jesus carried his cross to an excruciating death; "carrying one's cross" is not simply an inconvenience or hardship that people in relationships must occasionally endure.

The third point Jesus makes is to "count the cost," so you know what is needed and expected if you become a follower of Christ.

The fourth condition may need a comment: Be "salty" persons. That is, be persons who not only are preservatives for great values but also ones who give taste and zest to their relationships. No one wants to sit down to a dinner of salt. But a pinch of salt does wonders to a steak. Be a salty person. If you cannot measure up to this, do not become Jesus' disciple.

Luke 15:1-32. Luke presents us with one of his "twin" parables. Both have the same point. In this case the two parables are about a man (shepherd) who loses one of his sheep and a woman who loses one of ten silver coins. Friends, neighbors, and God rejoice when the lost are found.

Remind the group members again of Jesus' love of Scripture—the Law, the Prophets, and the Psalms. Many of his parables and teachings are based on biblical events, sayings, and idioms. The story of what we often call the good shepherd is one of these and reflects the two prophets Ezekiel and Isaiah. Ezekiel 34:15-16 says, "I myself will tend my sheep and have them lie down, declares the Sovereign LORD. I will search for the lost and bring back the strays. I will bind up the injured and strengthen the weak, but the sleek and the strong I will destroy." Isaiah 40:11 also describes the care of the shepherd for his sheep: "He tends his flock like a shepherd: / He gathers the lambs in his arms / and carries them close to his heart; / he gently leads those that have young."

Ask a group member to read the entire parable (Luke 15:3-7) aloud, perhaps after you have read the two prophetic passages from Ezekiel and Isaiah. Ask them to discuss the question, What is unique about the Lord God in contrast to other deities? (You might want to list the differences on a whiteboard, a chalkboard, or a large piece of paper.) One point you might want to include is that God is unique in that God seeks and searches for lost persons. God does not send angels after the lost; God seeks the lost, hoping to carry them over his shoulders or in his bosom to safety. The angels of heaven rejoice over even one sinner who repents.

So also the woman who loses one of her ten silver coins (a drachma)—meaning she loses a tenth of all she has—searches frantically until the lost coin is found and then calls in friends to celebrate. In the same way, there is great rejoicing in the kingdom of God when a person who was lost is found.

The concluding story of the lost son (15:11-32) is conditioned by Deuteronomy 21:17, which defines how one son (generally the older) receives the lion's share of the father's estate—two-thirds. The other gets one-third. In the parable the younger son asks for and is given his one-third of the estate prior to his father's death. This is an insult to the parent, as it implies that the father is considered dead by his son. The older son will inherit the remaining estate after the father's death. Read the parable aloud.

This parable is called "the greatest short story in the world." It beautifully describes how a "lost" son comes to his senses in a foreign land and returns to and is received by a caring, thoughtful father. The older son is just as lost as was the younger. He refuses even to refer to his brother as "my brother," preferring to say "this son of yours" to his father.

DIMENSION THREE:
WHAT DOES THE BIBLE MEAN TO ME?

The participants may discuss the following topic or use the material in the participant book.

Luke 14:12-14—An Invitation to the Banquet

Luke 14:23 points out the importance of a word, as well as words, in "compel them to come in" to the banquet. Coercion does not work. Augustine demanded that the heretics called Donatists return to the Catholic church. Augustine forced people into the faith of the most powerful persons. Thus we have the origin of the terrible Inquisition, with its use of the rack, thumb screw, and other varied tortures to force theological uniformity. In Jesus' story the emphasis is on the consequences to those who freely and willfully chose not to attend the great banquet. At no time did Jesus coerce, force, or compel persons to accept his point of view. To the contrary, he told parables, hoping to win people to his way of life.

Jesus searches for persons who "make every effort to enter through the narrow door" (13:24). The action is not forced on possible converts but is the result of setting our priority in life and where it will lead us. Few consider the future to which their choices are leading them. The ancient proverb is so true, "What I am to be, I am now becoming." The amount of our agonizing determines which road we take and what our choices lead us to become.

Luke 13:30 quotes Jesus as saying, "Indeed there are those who are last who will be first, and first who will be last." The Pharisees loathed "the poor, the crippled, the blind and the lame" whose role is reversed in the kingdom of God. These last become first because they are the ones who hear and respond to the message of Jesus.

The Conditions of Discipleship

Form four small groups and assign to each group one of the conditions of discipleship: (1) "Hate" family; (2) Carry your own cross; (3) Count the cost; (4) Be "salty."

Ask them to discuss what each of these conditions meant then and means now. (Is this different?) What are the greatest obstacles to fulfilling that condition? What aspects of your faithfulness make the condition doable for you? What more might you need to be or do to be more faithful in that condition?

Whoever can be trusted with very little can also be trusted with much, and whoever is dishonest with very little will also be dishonest with much (16:10).

THE USE AND ABUSE OF WEALTH

Luke 16–17

DIMENSION ONE: WHAT DOES THE BIBLE SAY?

Answer these questions by reading Luke 16

1. To whom does Jesus tell the parable about a rich man who employs a dishonest manager? (16:1)
   Jesus tells the parable to his disciples.

2. What is the manager accused of doing? (16:1)
   He is accused of wasting his master's possessions.

3. On confronting his manager, what does the rich man order him to do? (16:2)
   The rich man orders the manager to turn in the account of his management, for he can no longer be manager.

4. Why does the scheming manager call in his master's debtors and discount their bills? (16:4)
   The scheming manager decides to discount the bills of his master's debtors so that people will receive him into their houses when he is unemployed and needy.

5. For what does the master commend the manager? (16:8)
   The master commends the manager for his shrewdness.

6. If a person is dishonest in a very little, what might one expect of that person in a larger capacity? (16:10)

> *"Whoever is dishonest with very little will also be dishonest with much."*

7. Into what two periods does Jesus divide time? (16:16)

> *Jesus divides time into the time of the Law and Prophets until John and the time of the kingdom of God.*

8. Who lies at the rich man's gate? (16:19-20)

> *A beggar named Lazarus lies at the rich man's gate.*

9. What happens when Lazarus dies? (16:22a)

> *When Lazarus died, "the angels carried him to Abraham's side."*

10. What happens when the rich man dies? (16:22b-23)

> *The rich man dies, is buried, and goes to hell, where he is tormented.*

11. To whom does the rich man want Abraham to send Lazarus, and why? (16:27-28)

> *The rich man wants Lazarus to go to his father's house to warn the man's five brothers so they can avoid the rich man's fate.*

12. What is Abraham's response to the rich man? (16:31)

> *Abraham says, "If they do not listen to Moses and the Prophets, they will not be convinced even if someone rises from the dead."*

Answer these questions by reading Luke 17

13. What does Jesus say about the sin of causing others to sin? (17:2)

> *Jesus says, "It would be better for them to be thrown into the sea with a millstone tied around their neck than to cause one of these little ones to stumble."*

14. If a brother sins against you seven times in the day and turns to you seven times and says, "I repent," what must you do? (17:4)

    You must forgive him.

15. How do the disciples reply? (17:5)

    The disciples reply, "Increase our faith!"

16. Why does one not thank a servant who does what he or she is told to do? (17:9-10)

    One does not thank a servant for doing what is his or her legitimate labor.

17. As Jesus enters a village, he meets ten persons who have leprosy who ask for pity. What does he tell them? (17:14)

    Jesus tells the persons with leprosy, "Go, show yourselves to the priests."

18. As the persons who have leprosy go by, they are cleansed. Why does one person who had leprosy return and fall at Jesus' feet? (17:15-16)

    He returns to give Jesus thanks.

19. Which one of the ten persons who had leprosy thanks Jesus? (17:16-18)

    The man who is a foreigner, a Samaritan, thanks him.

20. What does Jesus say to Pharisees who ask when the kingdom of God is coming? (17:20-21)

    Jesus says that it is not "here" or "there," the "kingdom of God is in your midst."

21. What warning does Jesus give his disciples about the false teachers who say "Look there!" or "Look here!" when they yearn for the Son of Man? (17:22-23)

    Jesus warns them, "Do not go running off after them."

22. What lesson can one learn from "the days of Noah" and "the days of Lot" with regard to "the day the Son of Man is revealed"? (17:33)

"Whoever tries to keep their life will lose it, and whoever loses their life will preserve it."

DIMENSION TWO:
WHAT DOES THE BIBLE MEAN?

The Scripture for this lesson is divided into four themes:

1. Faithfulness in Administration (16:1-15)
2. The Gospel and Wealth (16:16-31)
3. Forgiveness, Faith, Grace, and Ingratitude (17:1-19)
4. The Kingdom of God (17:20-37)

Luke 16:1-15. The parable of the unjust manager is one of the more difficult of Jesus' stories to interpret. In terms of Dimension Two, "What does this parable mean?" we are to think of administrators and managers (of estates) from a Christlike perspective. Obviously, some attitudes and actions are not acceptable. God cannot, by God's nature, support dishonest conduct of his managers. Or can he? Does the end justify the means? Does Christ approve immoral actions when the consequences seem to be good? Some interpreters during the centuries have assumed that Jesus supported the dishonest manager because he was a clever schemer. Let us look closely at the story.

Jesus speaks to his disciples. He tells them that a rich man placed his large estate of several farms in the hands of a manager (steward). The wealthy owner learns that his manager is spending his money "like mad." The owner calls his manager before him and asks, "What is this I hear about you?" Apparently the manager admits by his silence the validity of the reports. So the owner orders him to turn in his various records. Still silent, but with a busy mind, the manager goes toward his home. He says to himself, *I know what to do so that those who owe my master will receive me joyfully in their homes when I am put out of my job as manager.*

The manager realizes he must act quickly before his debtors learn he has been fired. He summons his master's debtors one by one. He asks the first one, "How much do you owe my master?" He replies, "Nine hundred gallons of olive oil." The manager, wanting to win the debtor's gratitude, says, "Take your bill . . . and make it four hundred and fifty." (The debtor gets a windfall.) The manager asks the next farmer how much he owes for the large crop on his wheat field. He reports that he owes a thousand bushels of wheat. The manager says, "Take your bill and make it eight hundred."

The master, when he learns what his dishonest manager has done, commends him for his shrewdness. The master is in a difficult spot. If he calls his renters before him and admits that his manager has bested him, he will also have to admit that the debtors' enthusiastic acclaim of the manager's generosity and kindness is a fraudulent claim against his own character. At this point, the best course is to pretend to be the generous landlord who has reduced their rents. Meanwhile the scheming manager has won the favor of the farmers, since he pronounced the fine discounts.

By deliberately choosing a case from the field of human existence, Jesus addresses himself to human beings as they really are. Jesus cannot praise the dishonest manager for his immoral actions. He does acknowledge cleverness as a creditable attribute. Jesus says, "The people of this world are more shrewd in dealing with their own kind than are the people of the light" (16:8). The real point of this parable is about entering the kingdom of God. The coming of the kingdom of God remains wholly the act of God. The kingdom of God is a completely different world compared with all that is earthly, and in Jesus' view the kingdom of God is a gift of grace from God.

We all have heard people say, "He is a man of means." However, our concern focuses on worthy ends. Are the "means" (money, property, goods, things) being used for selfish purposes or for great and noble ends? We might ask, What makes for greatness? For the "people of the light," greatness is judged not by one's means but by the nobility of the ends.

Luke 16:14-15 gives a brief commentary about the Pharisees, whose major sin (as seen in the Gospels) is spiritual pride and religious arrogance. Little evidence exists to indicate that the Pharisees were dedicated to worshiping at the shrine of money. This charge could more readily be laid at the feet of the Sadducees, who were the truly wealthy and affluent Jews of Jesus' time. The Sadducees, the group of two hundred high priests of Jesus' time, all lived within the city of Jerusalem. They had beautiful homes of carved marble and enjoyed a fabulous income from taxes given to the temple.

The Pharisees' sins were pride in their obedience to the oral traditions of the elders and pride in their ostentatious piety. (They prayed three times a day on busy street corners, and they prayed longer prayers than the law required.) Perhaps Luke remembers hearing the loud clatter of coins as Pharisees cast their gifts into the offering boxes at the temple, contrasting with the almost silent tinkle of a widow's mite. Their love for money was subordinate to their love for recognition in pious giving to the Lord. Jesus said to them, "You are the ones who justify yourselves in the eyes of others, but God knows your hearts. What people value highly is detestable in God's sight" (16:15).

Luke 16:16-31. The Gospel of Luke divides history into two parts (16:16). The giving of the Law and its varied interpretations, plus great covenants and promises of God made to, by, and through the prophets, occurs until John.

Jesus begins the second period by preaching the good news of the kingdom of God. And "everyone is forcing their way into it" (16:16). Consider the feelings involved if your spouse, father or mother, or children put their love for Christ and God above their love for you. Consider the turmoil a pious Jew like Paul felt when he experienced the rending of his beloved law as the spirit of Christ led him to a much greater law—the law of love, faith, and hope in God as seen in the resurrected Jesus Christ. Many persons experience the turmoil and violence of rebirth.

An example of violence is noted in the pure and unadulterated irony of Jesus' words about those who are so dedicated to the written and unwritten (oral) law that "it is easier for heaven and earth to disappear than for [scribes and Pharisees to let] the least stroke of a pen to drop out of the Law" (16:17).

In the parable of the rich man and Lazarus (16:19-31), Jesus uses a personal name. The name *Lazarus* is the only proper name given in Jesus' parables. The rich man is clothed in purple and fine linen and feasts sumptuously every day. Ask group members to list what they know about Lazarus. (Work in small groups for five minutes; then share with everyone. Write the suggestions on a whiteboard, a chalkboard, or a large piece of paper.) Some ideas are these: He is a very poor man; he probably is an invalid, since he lies at the gate every day; his body is covered with sores that the dogs lick; his food is what falls from the rich man's table and is scooped up from the floor; and finally, he dies.

Contrast the deaths of the two men. Lazarus, the beggar, dies and is *carried by the angels to Abraham's side*. The rich man also dies and *is buried*. In hell the rich man, whose eyes had always focused on things on the earth, looks up and sees "Abraham far away, with Lazarus by his side." The rich man, who gave crumbs of pity from his floor to Lazarus, now requests that Lazarus give pity. He wants Lazarus to dip his finger in water and cool the rich man's tongue.

The parable has a poignant touch as the hearers recall that Sadducees do not believe in life after death. Perhaps this chasm is that to which Abraham refers when he says, "Between us and you a great chasm has been set in place, so that those who want to go from here to you cannot, nor can anyone cross over from there to us." The rich man then begs Abraham to send Lazarus to his five brothers to warn them, lest they too go to "this place of torment." The answer is this: "They have Moses and the Prophets; let them listen to them." That is, Read the Scripture! But the rich man pleads further, saying, "No, father Abraham, . . . but if someone from the dead goes to them, they will repent." Abraham's response is, "If they do not listen to Moses and the Prophets, they will not be convinced even if someone rises from the dead."

A group member may raise a question about life after death. In the Old Testament the Hebrew word *Sheol* is the name of the shadowy and gloomy place to which the spirits of persons go after death—as was the case with Samuel. (See 1 Samuel 28:8-19.)

The Jews began to think of Sheol (hell) as being divided into two distinct places: Gehenna and Paradise. Gehenna is the place that receives the unrighteous, such as the rich man in the above parable. In Gehenna those whose lives on earth were immoral and irreligious get their reward: everlasting punishment. In Paradise those whose lives were righteous and filled with faith are rewarded by being in a right relationship with Abraham, the founder of the faith, and, of course, with God. Persons on each side (Gehenna and Paradise) can see and hear one another, but they cannot cross over; for in between is a great chasm.

Mention to group members that people always want signs, the best of which (they say) is to see a person who has returned from the grave. Interestingly enough, Herod, who murdered John the Baptist, heard that Jesus was John the Baptist risen from the dead (9:7); yet Herod did not change his way of life.

Ask participants whether persons are redeemed by signs, by persuasive arguments that lead to decisions, or by either.

Another discussion possibility might be as follows: Was it foreordained that the rich man be condemned to Gehenna? What life choices might have changed his future? What determines our lot?

Luke 17:1-19. In this section we "string" four "pearls." In light of the above parable on rewards (Paradise or Gehenna), Jesus says it would be better for a person whose instructions lead one of these little ones to sin if a millstone were hung around his or her neck and he or she was thrown into the sea (17:2). The future life in Sheol is terribly bleak. What difference is there between the love of fine clothes and daily feasts and the search for truth? Help group members realize that raising questions about the meaning of parables is not a sin. We must raise questions; otherwise ignorance becomes the guide that misleads us.

If a brother or sister sins, we have several options we can pursue. We may (1) carry secret grudges; (2) complain to a third party; or (3), as Jesus suggests, lovingly rebuke him or her. If a person sins (particularly against us), we should help that person deal with the sin. For if sin is cultivated, it keeps persons from attaining the strongest, highest, and loveliest life. We sin if we do not help another deal with his or her sin.

If a person sins against us seven times a day and turns and says after each offense, "I repent," we must forgive him or her. Little wonder that the disciples turn in amazement and say, "Increase our faith!"

But how can we *forgive*? We must lay aside all claim to requital. We must pray for dissolution of our resentment. We must live with the offender in healing and creative love. As we forgive, the doors open; and love restores us to the abundant life.

Luke 17:7-10. In the parable of the servant and one's duty, Jesus makes the significant point that those who are truly committed to God always act out of the sense of "I ought." God does not owe us anything; we owe God. In formal ethics we might say that we act out of a dutiful will—with no room for pride or merit on our part: I ought to do this. "We are unworthy servants; we have only done our duty" (17:10).

Luke 17:11-19. Another "pearl" in our necklace of the jewels of the spirit is the story of the grateful Samaritan. To orient group members, give some background material by reporting on Leviticus 14:1-31, regarding the regulations for diseased persons at the time of ceremonial cleansing. Make the report short, being sure to mention the use of a live bird to symbolize the leprosy that has flown away from the healed person. The life of a person with leprosy was exceedingly painful and humiliating. For priestly tests of leprosy and its cures, see Leviticus 13. Until the diseased person was cleansed, he was to cover his upper lip and cry out, "Unclean! Unclean!" The person with leprosy lived outside the camp. The isolation; the loneliness; and the physical, psychological, and theological pain were excruciating.

Luke, a Gentile physician, seems to enjoy telling about the (only) two healings of leprosy—and especially the one with the foreigner (Samaritan) who is the only one of ten who returns to thank Jesus. Nine of the ten persons with leprosy are Jews. It is this tenth one, the Samaritan, who returns to Jesus praising God. We assume the other nine find a priest who will pronounce them clean. What did the nine tell the priest at the temple? Did they refer to Jesus as messiah, healer, or the unknown prophet? What do group members think? Did ingratitude warp the attitude toward Jesus of the nine persons cured from leprosy?

Suggest that we may find the ultimate meaning of this healing as we sympathize with the sufferers, especially with the foreigner, the Samaritan who praised God.

Luke 17:20-37. Apparently, some Pharisees are traveling with the disciples. Some may have marveled at the miracle of the healing, and perhaps the glory of the Samaritan's face stirs them to ask Jesus when the kingdom of God is coming. They are actually spectators already, but to "see" the King (Jesus Christ) of the Kingdom is beyond their spiritual abilities. Jesus again says the Kingdom does not come with observable signs (17:20). The specific signs in Nain and in Capernaum are all misleading. The only signs are those close at hand: The kingdom of God is in the midst of you: it is within you; it is among you. The yeast of the Kingdom is growing within and among persons. How easily we miss the meaning of this passage and substitute a search for fruitless signs. Jesus asks us not to waste our energies with such things. Jesus says, "The time is coming when you will long to see one of the days of the Son of Man, but you will not see it." He begs them, "Do not go running off after them." Accept Jesus.

DIMENSION THREE:
WHAT DOES THE BIBLE MEAN TO ME?

The group may discuss the following topics or one or more of the topics in the participant book.

Luke 17:11-19—Gratitude and Ingratitude

One of the major teachings of this lesson is the tragedy of ingratitude. When the Lord healed the ten men from their leprosy, his instructions were that they should go to the priest. When they left Jesus, they still had leprosy; it was while they were on their way that they were healed. Since the ritual cleansing was an important issue and since the men were already on their way doing just what Jesus had instructed, we may find it hard to blame the nine for ingratitude. Does not Jesus elsewhere criticize those who delay when they are told to follow his call? Yet the one returns for a word of thanks, and that is commendable.

Assuming the kingdom of God is in our midst—both within and among us—then we should regularly thank Jesus for standing among us in his risen power. This apparently is what the Samaritan man could see.

Luke 17:3-5—Increase My Faith

A challenging word comes from 17:3-5 when Jesus responds to the disciples' amazement that their faith should be such that they can forgive a sinner seven times a day for the same sin—assuming real repentance. They say, "Increase our faith!" Jesus responds that it is not the quantity of your faith but the quality of your faith that makes the difference. Who judges either the quality or the quantity of our faith? Is faith quantifiable? What are the signs of an "increased" faith?

What is impossible with man is possible with God (18:27).

10

THE KINGDOM OF GOD

Luke 18:1–19:44

DIMENSION ONE:
WHAT DOES THE BIBLE SAY?

Answer these questions by reading Luke 18

1. In the parable of the persistent widow, how often does Jesus say the disciples should pray? (18:1)

   "They should always pray and not give up."

2. What does the widow ask the judge to do? (18:3)

   She asks the judge to grant her justice against her adversary.

3. What word does Jesus use to describe the judge? (18:6)

   Jesus uses the word unjust *to describe the judge.*

4. Who are the two men who go into the temple to pray? (18:10)

   One man is a Pharisee, and the other is a tax collector.

5. In his prayer, what kinds of people does the Pharisee say he is not like? (18:11)

   He says he is not like robbers, evildoers, adulterers, and tax collectors.

6. What does the Pharisee do? (18:12)

   He fasts twice a week and gives a tenth of all he gets.

7. How does the tax collector pray? (18:13)

He stands at a distance and does not even look up to heaven and beats on his breast.

8. What does he ask God in his prayer? (18:13)

The tax collector asks God to have mercy on him, a sinner.

9. What does Jesus say when the people bring babies to him? (18:16)

Jesus says, "Let the little children come to me, and do not hinder them, for the kingdom of God belongs to such as these."

10. What does the ruler lack to inherit eternal life? (18:22)

The ruler does not have treasure in heaven.

11. How does Jesus answer the question "Who then can be saved?" (18:27)

Jesus says that "what is impossible with man is possible with God."

12. What will happen to Jesus? (18:32-33)

Jesus will be mocked, insulted, and spat upon. They will flog him and kill him, and on the third day he will rise.

13. What does Jesus say to the blind man when he asks to have his sight restored? (18:42)

Jesus tells him to receive his sight; his faith has healed him.

Answer these questions by reading Luke 19

14. Who tries to see Jesus in Jericho? (19:2-3)

Zacchaeus tries to see Jesus.

15. What does he do so he can see Jesus? (19:4)

He climbs into a sycamore-fig tree.

16. What does Jesus say to Zacchaeus when he says he will give half of his possessions to the poor? (19:9)

    Jesus says, "Today salvation has come to this house, because this man, too, is a son of Abraham."

17. What happens to the person who does not put the money in the bank to collect interest? (19:23-24)

    The mina is taken from him and given to the one who has ten minas.

18. What does Jesus ask two disciples to do at Bethphage? (19:30)

    Jesus asks them to find a colt, untie it, and bring it to him.

19. What are the disciples to say when someone asks them about taking the colt? (19:31)

    They are to say that "the Lord needs it."

20. What does the crowd of disciples say as Jesus rides the colt down the Mount of Olives? (19:38)

    They say, "Blessed is the king who comes in the name of the Lord! / Peace in heaven and glory in the highest!"

21. What does Jesus predict about Jerusalem? (19:44)

    Jesus predicts that Jerusalem and its people will be destroyed because they did not recognize the time of God's coming.

DIMENSION TWO:
WHAT DOES THE BIBLE MEAN?

The Scripture for this lesson is divided into four themes:

1. Parables on the Practice of Prayer (18:1-14)
2. Conditions of Entrance to the Kingdom (18:15-34)
3. Jesus in Jericho (18:35–19:27)
4. Jesus' Ministry in Jerusalem (19:28-44)

Luke 18:1-14. The key to the kingdom of God is prayer. However, we err when we assume that we can get anything we want if we only pray. Prayer is a way of learning the will of God, that we may then strongly assert it.

Jesus' parables sometimes use contrast rather than comparison. The parable of the widow and the judge is such a case. (See 18:1-8.) The judge is not interested in the widow's vindication. "Vindication" means to be cleared of suspicion, dishonor, or a charge of wrongdoing. The judge "neither feared God nor cared what people thought" (18:2). Again and again, the widow pesters him, attempting to wear him out. He finally gives in, takes her case to court, and sees that she gets justice.

Notice the principle of contrast: If an irreligious and socially insensitive judge will respond to a woman's persistence in presenting her requests, how much more readily will God respond to a person who persists in prayer? Through persistence the "pray-er" can rethink, rephrase, and reshape the content of the prayer. Persistence includes opportunity to think.

The parable of the Pharisee and the tax collector deals with spiritual or religious pride. A quotation from a rabbi who lived at the time the Gospel of Mark was being written, about AD 70, states, "I thank thee, O Lord, my God, that thou hast given me a place among those who sit in the House of Study, and not among those who sit at the street corners; for I rise early and they rise early, but I rise early to study the words of the Law, and they rise early to engage in vain things; I labor and they labor, but I labor and receive a reward, and they labor and receive no reward; I live and they live, but I live for the life of the future world, and they live for the pit of destruction" (quoted by S. M. Gilmour, in *The Interpreter's Bible*, Volume 8; Abingdon Press, 1952; page 308).

Jesus tells this parable to "some who were confident of their own righteousness and looked down on everyone else" (18:9). Two men went up to Herod's temple to pray, one a Pharisee and the other a tax collector for Rome. The Pharisee fasts twice a week—Mondays and Thursdays, though neither is required of him; and he tithes, not just of the produce of the land as required by the Torah, but "of all I get." His prayer expresses gratitude for his virtues: "I thank you that I am not like other people—robbers, evildoers, adulterers—or [looking over at the tax collector] even like this [despicable] tax collector." The Pharisee's self-confidence and self-satisfaction oozed all over his countenance. But the tax collector, standing far off from the sacred altar, beats his breast in remorse and prays, "God, have mercy on me, a sinner." It was a shock to all the Pharisees and teachers of the law present to hear Jesus conclude that the kingdom of God requires reversal of values and therefore of judgments. The sinners are among the saved; the ostentatiously pious become the sinners in need of salvation.

By the second century AD, many Christians fasted twice a week also—but on Wednesdays and Fridays! Their tithing habits often became legalistic too. They often fell into the same trap of self-righteousness. Keep in mind that *not all* Pharisees were self-righteous people. Many, as probably was Jesus' brother James, were sincere, loved God, and served people.

Luke 18:15-34. The Jews believed that the fathers (not the mothers) were responsible for teaching the faith to their children. (See Deuteronomy 6:4-12.) Obviously, many mothers assumed those responsibilities, however. On their children's first birthdays, fathers would take their offspring to an outstanding rabbi for his blessing of their infant. Luke states, "People were also bringing babies to Jesus for him to place his hands on them" (18:15). "Place his hands on" meant blessing them. Mark says "little children" were brought to Jesus too (Mark 10:13). Jesus loved them; he embraced them and welcomed the children as those whom God would wish to have in the Kingdom. "Anyone who will not receive the kingdom of God like a little child will never enter it" (18:17). Trust is the absolute essential of faith.

In the experience with the rich ruler, Jesus admits that things of this world easily become barriers to a wholehearted devotion to the cause of God. The ruler is imprisoned by wealth. He says he is pious; he has honestly and earnestly obeyed all the written and oral laws of the Torah from his youth. Although he has mastered the letter of the Law, perhaps the import and the spirit of the Law have not yet mastered him, however. "Jesus looked at him and loved him" (Mark 10:21). But one thing he still lacks: Though wealthy, he has no treasure in heaven. Jesus tells him to sell all he has and distribute it to the poor. "Then come, follow me." But the rich ruler becomes sad, for he cannot part with his earthly treasures. You might ask group members: Does God require all persons to sell all they have and distribute it to the poor? How about Zacchaeus? (See Luke 19:1-10.) Jesus does not tell him to do this. What is the difference between the two men? Also ask: What does God demand of your commitments?

Jesus comments, "How hard it is for the rich to enter the kingdom of God! Indeed, it is easier for a camel to go through the eye of a needle than for someone who is rich to enter the kingdom of God." Some rich persons are saved—depending on their attitude toward and their devotion to the things they possess. Jesus says, "What is impossible with man is possible with God" (18:27).

Peter, understanding the young man's difficult choice, shares the experience he and his brother Andrew had when they left their comfortable homes. (Peter was rich. He owned a large house in Capernaum, where Jesus stayed for many months; and Peter operated a big fishing business.) "We have left all we had to follow you!" Again call attention to Paul's statement in 1 Corinthians 9:5 that the disciples' wives accompanied them on their missions with Christ. Jesus must have felt it important for the men to have their wives with them. Some clearly do not have their wives or families with them, however. (See Luke 18:29.)

In verses 31-33, Jesus takes the Twelve aside and for the sixth time explains that they are going to Jerusalem where he must face physical, psychological, and spiritual pain. He will be mocked, spit on, flogged, and killed. But the sufferings are always told with the concluding word of confidence in Jesus' resurrection. You may want to write on a whiteboard, a chalkboard, or a large piece of paper the six references to his expectation of what will happen to him in Jerusalem: 9:22; 9:44; 12:50; 13:33; 17:24-25; 18:31-33. You might assign six persons to read these passages aloud.

Luke 18:35–19:27. Two events take place in the region of Jericho. As Jesus prepares to enter Jericho, a blind man stops him and asks for healing. And as Jesus prepares to leave Jericho, he sees Zacchaeus in a tree and invites himself to Zacchaeus's house.

This section of Scripture is a significant part of what is often called Luke's "Gospel of the Outcasts" (Chapters 15–19). The examples on the following list are either outcasts or a symbol of outcasts:

A stray sheep (15:3-7)
A lost coin (15:8-10)
A lost son (15:11-32)
A sick beggar (16:19-31)
A Samaritan man with leprosy (17:11-19)
A mistreated widow (18:1-8)
A despised publican (18:9-14)
A blind beggar (18:35-43)
A chief tax collector (19:1-10)

Ask for volunteers who will briefly review the passages as examples of "saved or found outcasts."

As Jesus enters and moves through Jericho, his mind focuses on anticipated events in Jerusalem within the next twenty-four hours. He teaches as he walks, with scores of followers seeking advantageous places from which to hear. Jesus would be talking loudly so all could hear.

The story of the blind man is very dramatic (18:35-43). The blind man is a beggar. He hears a multitude of people and the louder voice of a man teaching. He asks about what is happening. A friend says excitedly, "Jesus of Nazareth is passing by." Remembering stories he has heard of this amazing man, the blind man cries out loudly, "Jesus, Son of David, have mercy on me!" (This story is the only one in which both Luke and Mark [10:47-48] use the messianic title "Son of David.") The blind man wants to get Jesus' attention. Immediately, some people try to smother his voice, telling him to keep quiet. But he only cries louder, "Son of David, have mercy on me!"

Jesus stops his teaching and commands that the man be brought to him. Jesus asks what the beggar wants Jesus to do for him. The blind man says, "Lord, I want to see." Undoubtedly the phrase *Son of David* was meant to refer to the messianic dreams of great prophets such as Isaiah, who had said, " 'He will come with vengeance; / with divine retribution / he will come to save you.' / Then will the eyes of the blind be opened / and the ears of the deaf unstopped. / Then will the lame leap like a deer, / and the mute tongue shout for joy" (Isaiah 35:4b-6a).

"Immediately he [the beggar] received his sight and followed Jesus, praising God" (18:43). What does it mean for this formerly blind man to follow Jesus? Well, he goes with Jesus to the home of Zacchaeus, then to Bethany and to Jerusalem.

Before leaving Jericho, "the city of palm trees"—a jewel given to Cleopatra by Mark Antony, the showplace of Judah with its beautiful gardens of roses, a huge gymnasium, and lovely stone palaces—Jesus goes to the house of a chief tax collector. Jericho is a great business center with caravans crossing the area for markets around the world. Taxes are high and in abundance in Jericho. It has a commissioner of taxes, Zacchaeus, who has a group of tax collectors under his authority.

Zacchaeus climbs a tree because he cannot see Jesus, Zacchaeus being a man of small stature (19:3). Zacchaeus becomes a follower. Unlike the rich ruler, he wants more than anything else to be a follower of Jesus. He gives, without being told to do so, half of his large estate to the poor and declares he will give fourfold to any person he has defrauded. He is a great man, though considered unclean because he is an employee of Rome. As a follower, he goes far beyond the requirements of the Torah. Jesus declares, "Today salvation has come to this house, because this man, too, is a son of Abraham."

Zacchaeus's name comes from a Hebrew word meaning "righteous." *Righteous* seems to be an ill-fitting name for a chief tax collector. Yet, after hearing Jesus, Zacchaeus probably joins the multitude of followers as they climb the steep hills to Jerusalem.

Luke 19:28-44. The followers climb seventeen miles upward to Jerusalem, first arriving at Bethany. Near Bethany, Jesus asks two of his disciples to help him prepare to enter Jerusalem (on what we call Palm Sunday). Some persons believe that Jesus arranged to have a colt tied at a specific spot in the small village of Bethphage. The two disciples then go and untie the colt. The owner asks, "Why are you untying the colt?" And the disciples respond with the agreed-upon reply, "The Lord needs it." If one accepts this interpretation, one realizes that Jesus had a plan for publicly declaring his messiahship. He would enter Jerusalem riding on a colt, the foal of a donkey, as Zechariah prophesied (Zechariah 9:9). Jesus would come as the king of the kingdom of God—a man of peace, not of war; humble, not proud; with love, not with a demonstration of power.

Behind this careful planning for a dramatic and symbolic expression of his messiahship is the element of surprise for tens of thousands. During Jesus' ministry in Galilee, Samaria, Perea, Syrophoenicia, and Judah, Jesus has told those he healed to tell no one. Some, such as Legion, declared quite readily that Jesus was the long-awaited Messiah. But on the whole, Jesus minimized these expressions. Jesus knew that current ideas of what the Messiah and the nature of his kingdom would be like were very different from Jesus' understanding and ministry. Now, on Palm Sunday, Jesus declares to all that God has appointed him to be the Messiah, the Savior.

As planned, multitudes of followers (19:35-38) parade around Jesus, placing their garments on the colt and on the road. The "whole crowd of disciples" probably includes the seventy-two missioners who participated in the work through Samaria, the Twelve who were always with Jesus, and the crowd from Nazareth who came to see what their neighborhood young prophet was doing and saying and to express their pride in him.

As Jesus moves on the old Roman road from Bethphage to the Kidron Valley, he can see the beautiful city of Jerusalem. To see the city makes him weep, for her people do not know the meaning of peace; they know not the things that make for peace: love, honesty, unselfishness, and loyalty to God's covenants. They know only the ways of war—selfishness, racial and religious discrimination, hate, and greed.

In preparation for the Festival of the Passover, the great hymns of the week are being sung. Six psalms were repeated again and again. The hymns were called the Hallel, which includes Psalms 113–118. Psalm 118:26 is the well-known verse, "Blessed is he who comes in the name of the LORD."

Obviously, Jesus chooses this day as the specific time to declare publicly his messiahship. Notice that Luke omits any reference to the supposed messianic tie to David. (See Matthew 21:9 and Mark 11:10.) Why would he do so? Was it intentional? Ask group members to discuss this question in terms of its omission in Luke 19:38 (as contrasted with Matthew 21:9 and Mark 11:10).

Discuss at length the difference between Acts 1:3—"After his suffering, he presented himself to them and gave many convincing proofs that he was alive . . . and spoke about the kingdom of God"—and what the disciples say in Acts 1:6: "Lord, are you at this time going to restore the kingdom to Israel?" Even the disciples, let alone all the followers, have not understood what Jesus is saying when he says he comes to bring in the kingdom of God—*not the kingdom of Israel.* Pontius Pilate is not the only one who cannot understand what Jesus means by the Kingdom. And perhaps thousands (or more) today to not know the difference.

One significant and beautiful sentence in this account is Luke's report of the disciples crying out, "Blessed is the king who comes in the name of the Lord! / Peace in heaven and glory in the highest!" Luke begins his Gospel (chapter 2) with the birth of Jesus in relationship to a decree from Caesar Augustus of Rome. Both the baby Jesus and Caesar Augustus have a special message concerning peace on earth and glory in the highest (2:14).

Luke associates the reign of Augustus (31 BC–AD 14) with the birth of Jesus in an unusually subtle way. Augustus brought an era of peace to the Roman Empire beyond anything seen previously. The Roman Senate ordered that an altar to Pax Augustus be erected and consecrated in the Campus Marius. Peoples in the eastern Mediterranean world hailed Augustus as god and "savior of the whole world." Rome celebrated the birthday of this famous man by declaring, "The birthday of the god was the beginning of the good news to the world on his account" (*The Interpreter's Dictionary of the Bible,* Volume A–D; Abingdon Press, 1962; page 319).

Luke associates the birth of Jesus, the Messiah of the world, with the famous emperor who brought peace to an empire. Luke writes to Theophilus that the real savior of the world, the real giver of peace to the world, is the babe born in Bethlehem. Jesus will be hailed, not as emperor, but as the King of the kingdom of God, the One who is to come in the name of the Lord. When all persons of all countries acknowledge that Kingdom, we will all know "peace in heaven and glory in the highest!" (19:38). Against that background Jesus predicts the destruction of Jerusalem (19:41-44) because its people have not learned the way that leads to peace.

DIMENSION THREE:
WHAT DOES THE BIBLE MEAN TO ME?

The group may discuss the following topic or use the material in the participant book.

Right Motivation

Religion that abuses the nature and character of God may become the most destructive force in a community. Jesus knew his people were religious and sincere. But pride and arrogance can destroy that which God has hallowed. Faith is the thread of the woof that weaves the warp of life together into a brilliant and warm tapestry.

Jesus, after the Palm Sunday experience of declaring his messiahship publicly, goes to the temple. Isaiah had said, "My house will be called / a house of prayer for all nations" (56:7). Jesus finds bawling cattle; a stench that stifles the smell of incense, myrrh, and frankincense; and a market for the greedy who hypocritically pretend to be serving those who seek absolution of their sins. Jesus, in a rare fit of anger, overturns the tables of the money changers, chases the beasts from the temple area, and rebukes those who sell unblemished animals for the sins of others.

What "table" might Jesus overturn in your church or in your life? Jesus expressed great criticism of the pride and hypocrisy exhibited by some scribes and Pharisees. Current surveys of religion in the US show that church attendance and religious affiliation are (and have been) on the wane, as fewer young people feel the need for organized religion. What, do you think, either turns off or turns away potential adherents? What makes it difficult for you to feel motivated or included? What sort of radical hospitality might you and your church need to employ to welcome others in?

Heaven and earth will pass away, but my words will never pass away (21:33).

11
JESUS RESPONDS TO DIFFICULT QUESTIONS

Luke 19:45–21:38

DIMENSION ONE:
WHAT DOES THE BIBLE SAY?

Answer these questions by reading Luke 19:45–20:18

1. Whom does Jesus drive out of the temple? (19:45)

   Jesus drives out those who were selling sacrificial animals.

2. Who seeks to kill Jesus? (19:47)

   The chief priests, teachers of the law, and leaders among the people seek to kill Jesus.

3. What question do the chief priests, teachers of the law, and elders ask Jesus? (20:2)

   They ask, "Tell us by what authority you are doing these things. . . . Who gave you this authority?"

4. What question does Jesus ask them? (20:4)

   Jesus asks if the baptism of John was "from heaven, or of human origin."

5. In the allegory of the wicked tenants, what do the tenants do to the first servant? (20:10)

   The tenants beat the first servant and send him away empty-handed.

6. After sending the third servant to no avail, whom does the owner of the vineyard send? (20:13)

   The owner of the vineyard sends his son, whom he loves.

7. What do the tenants do to the owner's son? (20:15)

> *The tenants throw the son out of the vineyard and kill him.*

8. What will the owner of the vineyard do? (20:16)

> *The owner of the vineyard will kill the tenants and give the vineyard to others.*

Answer these questions by reading Luke 20:19–21:4

9. What does Jesus say to those seeking to trap him on the issue of paying taxes to Caesar? (20:24-25)

> *Jesus says, "Then give back to Caesar what is Caesar's, and to God what is God's."*

10. What question do the Sadducees ask Jesus about a woman who married seven brothers? (20:33)

> *The Sadducees ask, "At the resurrection whose wife will she be?"*

11. Why do the teachers of the law answer, "Well said, teacher"? (20:39-40)

> *Jesus' opponents could not come up with a response.*

12. Of whom are the disciples to beware? (20:46)

> *The disciples are to "beware of the teachers of the law."*

13. Why does Jesus say the poor widow put more in the treasury "than all the others"? (21:4)

> *Jesus says that the others contributed out of their wealth, but "she out of her poverty put in all she had to live on."*

Answer these questions by reading Luke 21:5-38

14. When Jesus tells them that one day the temple will be destroyed, what do the disciples ask? (21:7)

> *The disciples ask when these things will happen and what sign will indicate they are about to take place.*

15. When will be the time for the disciples to be witnesses? (21:12-13)

    The disciples are to bear testimony when they are persecuted, imprisoned, and brought before kings and governors for Jesus' sake.

16. Why do they not need to worry before answering questions? (21:15)

    Jesus will give them words and wisdom that no one can resist or contradict.

17. How will they save their lives? (21:19)

    By standing firm, they will save themselves.

18. When they see Jerusalem surrounded by armies, what has come near? (21:20)

    Jerusalem's desolation has come near.

19. What is Jesus' prediction about Jerusalem and her people? (21:24)

    "They will fall by the sword and will be taken as prisoners to all the nations. Jerusalem will be trampled on by the Gentiles."

20. When the Son of Man returns, where will they see him? (21:27)

    "They will see the Son of Man coming in a cloud with power and great glory."

21. What will all the physical changes in the earth mean? (21:28)

    The physical changes in the earth will mean that redemption is drawing near.

22. When the trees sprout leaves, what will they know? (21:29-31)

    They will know "the kingdom of God is near."

23. What does Jesus say will not pass away? (21:33)

    Jesus says, "My words will never pass away."

24. What is Jesus doing during the day? (21:37)

Every day he is teaching in the temple.

DIMENSION TWO:
WHAT DOES THE BIBLE MEAN?

The theme for this session deals with how Jesus responds to difficult questions. Jesus' answers to five basic questions show a brilliant logician, a masterful Bible student and theologian, and a man of unprecedented authority.

Jesus is first asked by what authority he teaches, heals, and interprets Scripture. The second question is clearly politically motivated: Should dedicated Jews pay their annual tax to Caesar? The third question asks if Jesus really believes in life after death, with its implications for marriage after the death of a spouse. The fourth question, raised by Jesus himself, deals with the relationship of the concept of the son of David with his understanding of the meaning of messiahship. The fifth question deals with how faith relates to prophetic ideas. You may want to list these five questions on a chalkboard, a markerboard, or a large piece of paper prior to the session.

The Scripture is divided into three themes:
   1. Opposition of the Sanhedrin (19:45–20:18)
   2. Three Basic Questions (20:19–21:4)
   3. Events That Mark the End of the Age (21:5-38)

Luke 19:45–20:18. The Sanhedrin was furious at Jesus' cleansing of the temple. This cleansing was particularly resented by the chief priests, who formed the largest group within the seventy-one members of the Sanhedrin. (Annas, an ex-chief priest, was a powerful member.) The chief priests were the authorities in matters of temple ritual and worship. They validated animals brought to the religious festivals for sacrifice to God.

The house of Annas (whose son-in-law was the current chief priest, Caiaphas) owned all the booths that sold sacrificial animals. The priests were given the power to decide which animals were unblemished and worthy of being used as sacrifices to God. If a priest saw an animal that, for example, James and John (sons of Zebedee) of Galilee brought to Jerusalem, and it had a bit of black wool on his otherwise all-white body, he (always a male) was declared unworthy. The priest was glad to purchase the sacrificially worthless animal and substitute a perfect one from Annas's herd for a handsome profit. This practice extended to lambs, bullocks, pigeons, and goats.

Another lucrative business was the changing of coins from foreign countries into the coins of the temple. Jews from throughout the world came to Jerusalem to worship. This worship involved offering sacrificial animals and changing the coins of their native land for the coins of the temple in Jerusalem.

When Jesus drives out these persons who are gaining wealth through their monopoly on the sales of unblemished animals and when he overturns the tables of the money changers, he upsets the lucrative business of the priests. Jesus holds a view similar to the prophet Amos of 750 BC. You might want to read Amos 5:21-24 aloud. These verses express Amos's anger toward those who place acts of worship (rituals, festivals, creeds) above a life of worship.

Jesus would readily agree with Amos that moral action rates higher than participation in religious holidays. Jesus' concern that persons accept and do the will of God in everyday life, even in the marketplace, and that they help others worship, identifies him as a prophet. No wonder the priests wanted to get rid of Jesus, who was much too prophetic, not only in his thoughts but also in his actions.

In this highly emotional setting, we begin this lesson. Luke mentions that the chief priests, the teachers of the law, and leaders (the elders) of the people are trying to destroy Jesus. (See 19:47.) These three groups form the Sanhedrin. They hold not only religious power but also the money purses of Judaism. The Sanhedrin "could not find any way to do it, because all the people hung on his words."

While in Galilee, Jesus is under the political authority of Herod Antipas. However, as a Jew, Jesus is under the religious authority of the Sanhedrin. The Sanhedrin, under the leadership of the priests whose purses are affected most, seeks ways to trap this great teacher and concerned religious leader, Jesus of Nazareth. Apparently, a committee of the three groups comes to Jesus to entrap him. They say, "Tell us by what authority you are doing these things. . . . Who gave you this authority?" (20:2).

Ask group members to suggest ideas that fall under the category of "these things."

Some possible answers are as follows: healing miracles, such as the blind beggar, the persons with leprosy, or Zacchaeus, who found a new wholeness when Jesus visited his home; Jesus' riding on a lowly donkey on Palm Sunday; the cleansing of the temple to rid the sacred place of greed and the exploitation of the poor. No wonder members of the Sanhedrin met to plot the arrest and death of this political upstart, Jesus, the so-called Messiah.

By what authority does Jesus do "these things"? He does them by the same authority that John had when he baptized persons in the Jordan: by the authority of God. Jesus knows their minds, and he knows what motivates their question. Jesus employs an often-used method of rabbinical teaching by posing a counter question to the question. The answer to the counter question is often suggestive of the answer to the initial question. Jesus asks them if the baptism of John was from heaven or from human beings. Now the priests are trapped. If they say that John baptized because of a command from heaven (that is, from God), then they acknowledge that John's proclamation of the coming Messiah is true—and this may be he who stands before them. If they say John baptized by human authority, the people will stone them because the people believe John is a prophet. They talk together and finally answer that they do not know whence it was. Their failure to answer the counter question enables Jesus to say, "Neither will I tell you by what authority I am doing these things" (20:8).

The Sanhedrin finds itself judged as invalid. The attack to paralyze Jesus' mission is itself paralyzed. But these unwholesome leaders are not yet finished. They remain in the crowd; and

Jesus addresses his next story to them, which is in the form of an allegory. Allegories are stories with surface meanings that represent deeper truths. In this allegory (Luke 20:9-19), each object or person has a current counterpart. The owner represents God, the tenants are the Jewish leaders entrusted with God's work, the servants are the prophets, and the beloved son is Jesus. Even from Old Testament times, the vineyard itself is Israel. (See Isaiah 5:1-7.)

Jesus addresses the allegory to the members of the Sanhedrin, who have just asked their impertinent question about authority. Now he tells them how disgusted God is with their leadership and that God will take their responsibilities away from them. They will be destroyed. With this in mind, you might want to tell or read the story. It goes like this:

Jesus tells the representatives of the Sanhedrin an allegory, which would apply directly to their own lives. A man (God) decides to leave the area for a long time. Not wanting to sell the land, the owner secures tenants (the religious leaders) who agree to pay him the customary amount. "At harvest time" (when the time came to collect his rent in kind—about five years according to Leviticus 19:23-25), the owner sends his servants (the prophets) for some of the fruit of his land. Three times he sends his servants; but each is beaten, treated shamefully, and sent away. Then the owner (God) sends his "son, whom I love" (Christ), hoping they will respect him. But the tenants plot and kill him, hoping to gain the inheritance. What will the owner of the vineyard do to the unworthy tenants? He will destroy them.

When the representatives of the Sanhedrin hear this, they say, "God forbid!" But Jesus looks at them and raises the question of God's judgment on them. He refers to Psalm 118:22 ("The stone the builders rejected / has become the cornerstone") and Isaiah 8:14-15 ("He will be . . . / a stone that causes people to stumble. . . . / Many of them will stumble; / they will fall and be broken"). Just so will judgment come to the immoral religious leaders of the Sanhedrin who do not accept Jesus as the Messiah.

Remember that the conditions indicated in this passage of Scripture reflect the period of time when Luke wrote. He is describing what the early church thought of the actions of the Sanhedrin against Jesus and how the early church soon accepted the rejected stone as the capstone of faith. (See Acts 4:11; 1 Peter 2:6-8.)

Luke 20:19–21:4. The teachers of the law and chief priests are aware that Jesus "had spoken this parable against them" (20:19). "Keeping a close watch on him, they sent spies, who pretended to be sincere. They hoped to catch Jesus in something he said, so that they might hand him over to the power and authority of the governor" (20:20). In 20:19, Luke observes that the teachers of the law and chief priests "looked for a way to arrest him immediately. . . . But they were afraid of the people." Unable to arrest him, they want to take hold of what he said. What is the difference between arresting him and catching him in an incriminating remark? Perhaps group members would have some suggestions. Would Jesus have been aware of the two attitudes of these schemers from the Sanhedrin?

Both Matthew (22:16) and Mark (12:13) mention that the Sanhedrin included some Herodians in the group, who were sent to spy on Jesus. The Herodians were influential Jews who maintained good relations with the house of Herod. They feared revolt by messianic leaders, and they were concerned about the Sanhedrin's claims that Jesus was a revolutionary.

The spies from the Sanhedrin present their carefully worked-out question to Jesus, "Is it right for us [Jews] to pay taxes to Caesar or not?" Explain that an annual tax (tribute) was paid by every male from age fourteen to sixty-five and by women from age twelve to sixty-five. The tax was relatively low, a denarius, a day's wage for a laborer. The tax is less a matter of finance than of religion. For many Jews, paying the tribute to Caesar seemed to be an acknowledgment of a king other than the Lord God.

If Jesus answers, "Yes, pay the tax," many Jews would say that Jesus recognizes Caesar as his king, which contradicts their theological claim that only God is the king of the Jews. If Jesus answers, "No, do not pay the tax," then he can be accused of treason, of encouraging a revolt against Caesar.

Jesus asks for a coin that bears on one side the image of the reigning Caesar. Jesus says in effect, Give to Caesar what has Caesar's image on it and to God that which has God's image on it. (Ask a group member to read Genesis 1:27 aloud.)

Jesus uses logical argument. Jesus also deals with the issues; he does not avoid the questions. He says yes, pay the tax levied by and for Caesar; and give to the King of kings what he has demanded, a committed life. Primary allegiance belongs to God. Caesars, czars, and kaisers come and go; but God and God's rule are forever.

The Sadducees (priests) raise another question in their attempt to catch Jesus in their net of words. Ask two persons to roleplay this event. Keep in mind that the Sadducees accepted only the Torah (the first five books of the Bible) and did not believe in the doctrine of life after death held by Pharisees. Perhaps the Sadducees address Jesus in scornful voice. They think they have the last word on doctrine, since Moses ordered them to teach the faith to all.

The conversation might go like this: The Sadducee speaks (with Genesis 38:8 and Deuteronomy 25:5-6 as background), "Teacher, Moses wrote that if a man's brother dies, leaving a wife but no children, the man must take the wife and raise up children for his brother. Now there were seven brothers; the first took a wife and died without children; and the second and the third brothers took her, dying without children. Likewise all seven brothers were married to her, leaving no children. Afterward the woman also died. In the resurrection whose wife will the woman be?"

The modern disciple responding for Jesus might say, "How do you know all seven went to heaven?" Jesus replies, "The people of this age marry and are given in marriage. But those who are considered worthy of taking part in the resurrection from the dead will neither marry nor be given in marriage, and they can no longer die; for they are like the angels. They are God's children. In this age, marriage is necessary to multiply the human race but is no longer necessary when persons become like angels and do not die any more." Jesus goes on to say that the Sadducees err in thinking that life after death does not exist. "God is the God of the living. You Sadducees, even with your limited canon of Scripture, know that God said to Moses, 'I am the God of your father, the God of Abraham, the God of Isaac and the God of Jacob'" (Exodus 3:6). The present tense, *I am*, denies that God's concern is over those once loyal souls who are now dead; God's concern is over those loyal servants who having died are with him now.

Once again, Jesus' understanding more than equals the teachings of the learned religious leaders of his day: "He [God] is not the God of the dead, but of the living, for to him all are alive" (20:38). No wonder some of the scribes say, "Well said, teacher!" Others no longer "dared to ask him any more questions" (20:40).

Jesus then raises a question with the Pharisees and Sadducees, both of whom honor and use the Psalms. The question deals with the identification of the Messiah with the son of David. In Luke 20:42, Jesus quotes Psalm 110:1.

In the Hebrew, the first line reads, "Yahweh [that is, the Lord God], says to Adonai [my liege, the king], sit at my right hand, till I make your enemies . . ." The poet has God talking to the Davidic king. For similar references of "my liege/my lord" (the king), see 1 Samuel 26:17; 1 Kings 1:13. The poet, writing a psalm for the enthronement of a new king, states that the king (of the Davidic dynasty) will be granted authority next to God. God will conquer his enemies, making them into a royal footstool. Judaism in the time of Jesus considered Psalm 110 a messianic psalm, as did early Christians—though it hardly matches the concept Jesus had of God's mission for the Messiah.

Luke wants to make it quite clear that Jesus the Christ is not a political leader. He is much more than the son of David, more than a descendant of the royal dynasty.

Jesus asks a difficult question of his hearers, "Why is it said [by the teachers of the law and chief priests] that the Messiah is the Son of David?" Jesus wants his hearers to know that he is indeed a descendant of David; but he wants to be known as the Son of God, a different kind of Messiah than David. Jesus is raising a significant question—not of genealogy, but of spiritual and moral sonship.

After these questions, Jesus apparently sits down on the temple pavement to rest. He looks up and sees the rich putting their gifts into the treasury.

The priests were in charge of collecting, counting, and using the monetary gifts made at the temple. The priests had thirteen basic items that made up their ongoing budget—such as costs for incense, wood for sacrifices, equipment for water, and so forth. So they developed a system of thirteen trumpet-shaped receptacles to receive the money. Each person put his or her gift in the receptacle of his or her choosing. Jesus watches the ostentation of the rich Sadducees (priests) and Pharisees as they loudly clang the trumpet-shaped receptacles with their metal coins. He also sees a poor widow who puts in two copper coins (leptons, worth one-tenth of a penny)—so small they can hardly be heard! Though small in size, her gift is of more value than all the gifts of the rich. "All these people gave their gifts out of their wealth; but she out of her poverty put in all she had to live on" (21:4). The greatest gift consists of that which costs the giver most and of the sacrificial generosity with which it is given.

Luke 21:5-38. You may want to write on a whiteboard, a chalkboard, or a large piece of paper "Four theological/biblical concepts." The first theological concept is that Jesus predicted the destruction of the temple (and Jerusalem).

Herod the Great began construction of the temple in 20 BC; it was not finished when it was destroyed in AD 70 by Titus. The temple was a beautiful building set in the center of a thirty-five-acre court. It was built of fitted white marble stones covered with huge plates of heavy gold.

Golden spikes rose on all sides of the roof to a height of 165 feet. The back of a large porch had gold-covered doors, with Babylonian tapestry of purple, blue, crimson, and gold depicting the heavens. Above it was the symbol of Israel: a golden vine. On a bright morning, looking from Olivet, a person could not look at the temple's beauty; for it reflected the sun.

During the past week, Jesus heard some people boasting of the temple's beauty. He had previously wept over Jerusalem because its people knew not the things that make for peace. Now Jesus predicts its destruction. When Luke wrote his Gospel, the temple had been destroyed for a little over a decade. (Luke wrote about AD 85–90.)

The second theological concept Jesus raises is the nature of time. Many Jews considered "the present age" evil and unredeemable (until God or God's Messiah came). Eventually, "the day of the Lord" would come. (Read Isaiah 13:10-13 and Amos 5:18-20 to group members. These passages give us the imagery of the stars, the sun and moon, the shaking of the heavens and earth in the days of God's wrath.) These two prophets give background for several of Luke's verses (21:9, 11, 25-26). These events usher in "the age to come," the golden age of God's rule and Jewish supremacy.

The third concept is the second coming of Jesus in a "cloud," reminiscent of God's coming to Moses at the tent of meeting in the cloud of God's presence. Luke 21:7-9, 27-28 includes many understandings of the day of the Lord.

The fourth concept deals with persecution. (See 21:12-19.) Luke probably thought of these verses as he recalled Peter and Paul's imprisonments. He includes their experiences in the Book of Acts.

DIMENSION THREE: WHAT DOES THE BIBLE MEAN TO ME?

Luke 20:41-44—The Son of David

Let us return to the question Jesus raises about the Messiah being David's son (Luke 20:41-44); that is, who is this man Jesus? Jesus raises this question because he wants his listeners (the group from the Sanhedrin) to acknowledge his divine appointment to messiahship. In the Fourth Gospel, Pilate states, "Here is the man!" (John 19:5) and "Here is your king" (John 19:14). In Matthew's Gospel, Pilate asks, "What shall I do, then, with Jesus who is called the Messiah?" (Matthew 27:22). Luke quotes Jesus as asking the disciples, "Why do you call me, 'Lord, Lord,' and do not do what I say?" (Luke 6:46).

The question is still very relevant: Who is this man of the genealogy of David (descended from David) whose views are often diametrically opposed to the beloved King David? Jesus was not the kind of king of Israel that the psalmist described in Psalm 110. Jesus asks the religious leadership of Jerusalem to rethink the meaning of the messianic hope, to reconsider his teachings and lifestyle cognitively, not emotionally. Does Jesus reflect God's Spirit? Is Jesus akin to God?

The End of the Age

Consider the four concepts noted in the commentary on Luke 21:5-38:

- The prediction of the destruction of the center of worship life

- The nature of time: the present, evil age versus the transformed age to come

- The return of Jesus

- Persecutions

There have been many prophetic warnings through the years that the world is in the throes of the end of the age (during the world wars, for example). The current turmoil in the world today certainly has alarming elements consistent with the End times—natural disasters around the world, growing events of terrorism, divisions and polarization within nations and the church, and so on. What do you make of these signs and of the biblical warnings about the End? Regardless of whether the End times are beginning, the world is in turmoil. In the face of such global and seemingly intractable problems, what can one Christian do? one church? one religious group?

We have found this man subverting our nation. He opposes payment of taxes to Caesar and claims to be Messiah, a king (23:2).

JESUS FACES HIS DISCIPLES AND ACCUSERS

Luke 22:1–23:25

DIMENSION ONE: WHAT DOES THE BIBLE SAY?

Answer these questions by reading Luke 22

1. As the Festival of the Passover draws near, what group of persons plots to get rid of Jesus? (22:2)

The chief priests and the teachers of the law plot to get rid of Jesus.

2. To whom does Judas go to betray Jesus? (22:4)

Judas goes to the chief priests and officers of the temple guard to betray Jesus.

3. How do Peter and John know where Jesus and the disciples will observe the Passover meal? (22:10-12)

They are to look for a man carrying a jar of water and to follow him to whatever house he enters. Then they are to ask the owner for the use of the guest room where the Teacher may eat the Passover with his disciples. The homeowner will show them a large upper room, furnished, where they are to make preparations.

4. After Jesus gives thanks for the wine, he says he will not drink wine until some great event occurs. What is this great event? (22:18)

Jesus will not drink "from the fruit of the vine until the kingdom of God comes."

5. As they celebrate the Passover, where is Judas? (22:21)

Judas sits at the table with all the disciples.

6. How does Jesus deal with the disciples' dispute about who is the greatest among them? (22:26)
Jesus says, "The greatest among you should be like the youngest, and the one who rules like the one who serves."

7. What does Jesus tell Peter will happen before the rooster crows this day? (22:34)
Peter will deny knowing Jesus three times.

8. What does Jesus ask of God in his prayer at Gethsemane? (22:42)
Jesus prays that God will "take this cup" from him.

9. What does Jesus say when Judas draws near to kiss him? (22:48)
Jesus says to Judas, "Judas, are you betraying the Son of Man with a kiss?"

10. What is Jesus' reaction when one of his disciples tries to protect him with a sword? (22:50-51)
Jesus says, "No more of this!"

11. What does Jesus say to the chief priests, officers of the temple guard, and elders? (22:52)
Jesus asks them why they are coming after him with swords and clubs when he has been with them every day in the temple courts—and they never laid a hand on him. He asserts that it must be because they were waiting for their hour—when darkness reigns.

12. Where do they take Jesus? (22:54)
They lead Jesus to the high priest's house.

13. On what three occasions does Peter deny knowing Jesus? (22:56-60)
1. A servant girl sees Peter as he sits in the light of the fire, and says, "This man was with him." Peter denies it.
2. Later someone else sees Peter and says, "You also are one of them." Peter denies it again.
3. An hour later another says, "Certainly this fellow was with him, for he is a Galilean." Peter states emphatically, "I don't know what you're talking about!" Then Peter hears the rooster crow.

GENESIS to REVELATION **LUKE**

14. When the rooster crows, who turns and looks at Peter? (22:61)
    The Lord turns and looks at Peter.

15. What do the men who hold Jesus in custody do to him? (22:63-65)
    The men mock him, beat him, and insult him. They also blindfold him and demand, "Prophesy! Who hit you?"

16. When day comes, where does the council of elders take Jesus? (22:66)
    At daybreak, Jesus is taken from the house of the high priest and led to the council of elders, scribes, and chief priests—the Sanhedrin.

17. What does the Council ask of Jesus, and what is his reply? (22:67-69)
    The Council asks, "If you are the Messiah, tell us." Jesus replies, "If I tell you, you will not believe me, and if I asked you, you would not answer."

18. With one voice they ask, "Are you then the Son of God?" What is Jesus' reply? (22:70)
    Jesus replies, "You say that I am."

Answer these questions by reading Luke 23:1-25

19. Where do the religious leaders take Jesus then? (23:1)
    The religious leaders take Jesus to Pilate.

20. What charges do the religious leaders bring to Pilate against Jesus? (23:2)
    They say that he is subverting the nation, opposing payment of taxes to Caesar, and claiming that he (Jesus) is Messiah, a king.

21. What question does Pilate ask Jesus? What is Jesus' response? (23:3)
    Pilate asks, "Are you the king of the Jews?" Jesus responds, "You have said so."

118

22. Learning that Jesus is a Galilean, to whom does Pilate send Jesus? (23:6-7)
    Learning that Jesus is a Galilean, Pilate sends Jesus to Herod, who is in Jerusalem at that time.

23. How do Herod and his soldiers treat Jesus? (23:11-12)
    Herod and his soldiers ridicule Jesus, mock him, dress him in an elegant robe, and send him back to Pilate.

24. Pilate offers to punish and release Jesus. For whose release does the crowd cry? (23:18-19)
    The crowd cries out, "Away with this man! Release Barabbas to us," naming an insurrectionist and a murderer.

DIMENSION TWO: WHAT DOES THE BIBLE MEAN?

The Scripture for this lesson is divided into four themes:

1. Jesus' Last Supper (22:1-23)
2. Jesus' Last Teachings to His Disciples (22:24-38)
3. Jesus in Gethsemane and His Arrest (22:39-65)
4. Jesus' Condemnation (22:66–23:25)

Luke 22:1-23. Today's Scripture is a part of the Passion narrative. The *Passion* generally refers to Jesus' sufferings prior to the cross, including the final time with his disciples at the Passover and his arrest in Gethsemane. Luke 22:1-23 includes the Sanhedrin's conspiracy against Jesus, Judas's breach of faith, preparation for the Passover, and a portion of the Last Supper.

The Sanhedrin was the chief judicial council, or supreme court of the Jews. It had seventy-one members (see Numbers 11:16) and was chaired by the high priest. Originally this body was composed of priests and Levites. Under Herod the Great, many Pharisees—none of whom were priests—became members of the Council.

The Pharisees represented a lay movement within the Council, and they were elected in parts. One person represented the legalistic party of Jesus' day (Shamai). He was paired off with a member of the liberal-thinking group (Hillel). The Pharisees' theological influence was tremendous, far exceeding that of the Sadducees.

Two days before the Festival of the Passover, some members of the Sanhedrin sought ways to arrest and kill Jesus. For fear of becoming ritually unclean and thus unable to participate in the Passover, they decided to wait until after the Passover. Meanwhile they plotted as to how they could achieve their goal.

Group members might like to discuss the question, Were those members of the Sanhedrin who were plotting to kill Jesus surprised when Judas came and offered to betray him? Do you suppose they questioned whether the timing was right, with only two days remaining before the Festival of the Passover? And what about the question of the right psychological moment for arresting Jesus, a popular teacher?

The Synoptic Gospels assume that Jesus celebrates the Festival of the Passover with his disciples. Jesus reserves an upper room, possibly in the home of Mark in Jerusalem. Jesus explains to Peter and John that, when they see a man carrying a water jar, they should follow him into the house he enters. When they see the householder, they are to ask for the guest room where Jesus is to celebrate the Passover. Peter and John find the guest room and prepare for the meal.

The Passover meal included roast lamb, bitter herbs, unleavened bread, and cups of wine mixed with water. The twelve disciples would have arrived for the Festival prior to sunset, at which time the Festival begins. (If a group member asks when Passover falls, be aware that the Gospel of John gives a different date for the Passover—one day earlier than Matthew, Mark, and Luke. John "corrects" the Synoptic Gospels by saying Jesus was crucified on the day the paschal lamb was slain. If so, then Jesus could not have celebrated the Passover with his disciples. We are accepting the date the Synoptic Gospels give for our study.)

The last supper Jesus eats with his disciples includes the hallowing of the Festival—asking God's blessing on the home as the Festival is celebrated. This "hallowing of the sacred day" is called Kiddush. The leader takes bread in his hands and praises God. Later he takes the wine and also praises God. Jesus uses this basic ritual as he breaks bread with his disciples at Passover. He gives new meaning to the old Passover ritual by saying, after he blesses God for the wine, "Take this and divide it among you." Then he takes bread, blesses God, and says, "This is my body." After supper he again takes the cup and says, "This cup is the new covenant in my blood, which is poured out for you."

Matthew and Mark write, "This is my blood of the covenant." Most Semites (such as Jews) of antiquity made covenants by smearing blood on the witnesses of or participants in the making of a covenant. (Refer to Exodus 24:6-8, where blood is used in making a covenant.) Perhaps Jesus had Jeremiah 31:31 in mind as he talked of his new covenant. The will of God will be chiseled not into tablets of stone, but into the hearts of persons. Remember that the heart (*lev*, in Hebrew) was considered the seat of motivation, will, and purpose. Asking Jesus to "come into my heart, Lord Jesus" means asking him to come into our motives, attitudes, dreams, and hopes. We move from low desires to the highest values in life when we permit the new covenant to become central in our lives. Such persons are witnessing with their "life's blood" on behalf of God's Messiah.

Paul is the earliest writer to describe the Lord's Supper (or Eucharist—meaning "thanks"). In 1 Corinthians 11:23-25 Paul adds, "Do this"—that is, perform or practice this. "Do this in remembrance of me." For Paul, the Lord's Supper is a time of remembering the Lord Jesus Christ. So Paul emphasizes three aspects: (1) the covenant is a new covenant (Jeremiah 31:31); (2) the words *do this* make it a Christian institution; (3) it is a time for remembering.

Some group members may have read Mark 14:20, which refers to the "one who dips bread into the bowl with me." The Passover required use of rather hard, thin, unleavened bread. This unleavened bread was broken and dipped into the sauce. You might want to refer to John 13:27, which states that Jesus gave Judas a piece of bread dipped in wine (a special sop). After Judas took the morsel, "Satan entered into him." Judas, refusing Christ's love, became demonic. Perhaps group members might illustrate the point: How does rejection of God's and Christ's love warp a person's character until a demonic spirit controls his or her life? Did Jesus' love still surround Judas as he left to betray his Master?

Luke 22:24-38. Learning that one of them will betray Jesus, the disciples begin to question one another. Strangely, the questioning then moves to a dispute "as to which of them was considered to be greatest." What would we think if a group of new bishops spent time debating among themselves as to who was the greatest?

Jesus' response to the question is, "The greatest among you should be like the youngest, and the one who rules like the one who serves." John's Gospel tells how Jesus takes a towel and a basin of water and washes his disciples' feet as a servant. The one who serves is greater than he or she who sits at table.

Jesus asks us to measure greatness, not by favors granted us, nor by merit earned, nor by position attained by self-seeking, but through our service to persons in Christlikeness. The model is the suffering servant who wins others to God by dedicated Christlike willingness to bear the burdens of others.

Luke 22:39-65. Luke, a Gentile, omits the last event in the observance of the Festival of the Passover: They sing a hymn. It would have been one of the six Hallel ("praise the Lord") psalms in the Old Testament, which was sung by all Jews as they celebrated the Passover that night. These psalms state God's mighty acts in Israel's behalf because of his steadfast love for Israel. Psalm 118 would reflect Jesus' immediate needs before God.

Surely the singing of the disciples bolstered Jesus. Perhaps they hummed as they left the upper room to go a few hundred yards to the garden of Gethsemane. Here Jesus leaves his disciples and goes to pray several yards farther up the terraced grove of olive trees. Jesus prays with the hope that God will "take this cup" from him. However, Jesus will follow God's will regardless of consequences. He would suffer the brutalities heaped upon the suffering servant (Isaiah 53) knowing that as he maintains good will, mercy, kindness, unselfishness, and hope, he will be God's man, living as God yearns for human beings to live. Jesus will demonstrate as never before what God wants human beings to be, even suffering and dying for sins he did not commit. He will die as he lived—a life that reflected the very life of God in attitudes, motives, disposition, thought-life, humility, mercy, and even judgment against evil.

Jesus prays to God in Gethsemane, not attempting to change God's will, but attempting to *know* God's will. When he knows God's will, he will assert it, even to the point of death. Gethsemane is a time, not so much of submission to the will of God, but of strong assertion of God's will. After Jesus concludes his prayer with a victorious conviction, he can take what will come to him, even betrayal by one of the Twelve and the eventual tortures of a cross.

You might want to discuss with group members the question: What did Jesus receive from prayer? Write answers on a whiteboard, chalkboard, or large piece of paper. Perhaps the most important thing Jesus received from prayer was God. Immanuel, God was with him. Nothing could separate him from the love and presence of God. And what did God receive from Jesus' prayer life? (Let group members make suggestions.) God got a man of God's own choosing, God's anointed Son, the Messiah.

Judas comes, guiding the captain of the temple guards to the place where Jesus is. Luke says Judas starts to kiss him; but Jesus stops him with a question, "Judas, are you betraying the Son of Man with a kiss?"

The eleven disciples are ready to fight on Jesus' behalf. Jesus curtly responds to their militant attitudes and actions: Enough of this! And his would-be defenders soon leave him, not knowing what to do with a Messiah who will not fight for his rights. They are frustrated and are like sheep without a shepherd.

Jesus asks the chief priests, officers of the temple, and elders why they come to him at night with swords and clubs. They have seen and listened to him teach the multitudes during the daytime, yet they did not lay a hand on him. "But this is your hour—when darkness reigns."

So they lead Jesus away from Gethsemane, across the Kidron Valley to the palace of Caiaphas in the south of Jerusalem. His various trials will soon begin.

Luke 22:66–23:25. You might want to explain the power structure of the chief priests, who play a great role in the Sanhedrin. Before Jesus' time, the high priest was chosen from the small but wealthy families who could trace their lineage back to Zadok, one of two chief priests appointed by David and the legitimate priest under Solomon. But in Jesus' time, Rome appointed the high priest and generally chose a man whose strain was not pure blood from Zadok.

Five powerful, wealthy families held the office of high priest in Jesus' time: the families of Boethus, Annas, Phabi, Camithus, and Cantheras. All were illegitimate priests. Annas headed up a strong clan. He was high priest from AD 6 to 14. Annas used his political power to see that five of his sons, his son-in-law Caiaphas, and later his grandson Jonathan held this powerful position of authority and wealth.

After Jesus' arrest in Gethsemane, the temple officers take him to the home of the high priest Caiaphas, son-in-law of the powerful Annas. Caiaphas, as high priest, is the head of the Sanhedrin, some of whose members are plotting to kill Jesus. But it is not yet daybreak, so the Sanhedrin cannot meet. Meanwhile, Peter three times denies knowing Jesus, the Galilean. The men who are holding Jesus mock him and beat him. They blindfold him and ask him to "prophesy" who is striking him on the face.

At daybreak, the members of the Council meet, and Jesus is led into their session (22:66). Caiaphas probably opens the session, stating the name of the person who is on trial for alleged blasphemy. Everyone is interested in Jesus' answer to the following question: "If you are the Messiah, tell us." Jesus does not answer yes or no. He says, "If I tell you, you will not believe me, and if I asked you, you would not answer." (So why should I answer anything?)

Jesus then says, "From now on, the Son of Man [referring to himself] will be seated at the right hand of the mighty God." The logical conclusion leads to the final question, "Are you then the Son of God?" Jesus responds, "You say that I am."

Though Jesus' response is equivocal, the Sanhedrin take it to mean that Jesus has admitted publicly that he is the long-awaited Messiah, the Christ. The Sanhedrin members ("the whole assembly," 23:1), then arise from their appointed seats in the Council and bring Jesus to Pilate for his judgment. Not all members of the Council draw the same conclusions. For example, Joseph of Arimathea is a secret disciple of Jesus. He later asks Pilate for Jesus' body to give it a proper burial, and Pilate agrees. After Jesus' death, "Nicodemus, the man who earlier had visited Jesus at night . . . brought a mixture of myrrh and aloes, about seventy-five pounds" (John 19:39). Paul knew some members of the Council, such as Gamaliel (Acts 5:34), who later cautions Council members that "you will only find yourselves fighting against God" (Acts 5:39). The ringleaders of the inner group who want to destroy Jesus include priests, Pharisees, and teachers of the law.

The plotters within the Sanhedrin want Pilate to condemn Jesus by confirming their decision of guilty (of blasphemy). They do not want Pilate to consider the case and decide by way of examination of the evidence. The plotters accuse Jesus, saying, "We have found this man subverting our nation. He opposes payment of taxes to Caesar and claims to be Messiah, a king." Pilate asks Jesus, "Are you the King of the Jews?" They take Jesus' "You have said so" as affirmative.

The witnesses generalize about Jesus' attitudes and his teachings, but no one names a specific Roman law he has violated. Pilate can find "no basis for a charge against this man" (23:4). The chief priests say that Jesus stirs people up with his teachings "all over Judea. . . . He started in Galilee and has come all the way here." Immediately, Pilate thinks of a way out—send Jesus to Herod Antipas, tetrarch of Galilee, who is in Jerusalem for the Festival of the Passover. Let Herod Antipas try Jesus and sentence Jesus, a citizen of Galilee.

So Herod Antipas faces Jesus. He knows many things Jesus is saying and is glad for this chance to see him. But Jesus does not respond to his governor's questions. Jesus gives no signs and works no miracles for Herod. The result is that Herod and his soldiers treat Jesus contemptuously and mock him. After Herod Antipas dresses Jesus in "an elegant robe," he sends this citizen of his own tetrarchy back to Pontius Pilate for him to deal with.

Pilate and Antipas, who have previously disagreed, become friends. On Jesus' return to the procurator's residence (the Tower of Antonia, just northwest of the temple area), Pilate calls the plotters from the Sanhedrin and the people before him. Again Pilate declares Jesus innocent of all charges. He declares his decision to punish and release Jesus.

The frenzied crowd shouts for the release of an insurrectionist named Barabbas, who has committed murder. Pilate, apparently afraid of a mob scene, releases the insurrectionist, but "surrendered Jesus to their will" (23:25). Thus through the cowardice of a procurator of Judah and the hysteria of the populace created by some evil forces within the Sanhedrin, the Messiah (Christ) moves toward Golgotha.

DIMENSION THREE:
WHAT DOES THE BIBLE MEAN TO ME?

The group may discuss the following topic or use the material in the participant book.

Luke 22:13-30—The Last Supper and Greatness

Immediately after the Lord's Supper and before going to Gethsemane, a dispute arises among the disciples as to which of them is to be regarded as the greatest (22:24-30). Jesus sees the dangerous seduction of power. Following Jesus involves abandoning the good things of this world and enduring persecution when it is necessary to preach the kingdom of God. In the realm of morality, beauty, truth, and religious faith, the followers of Jesus will sit as persons of authority. They will help persons understand what is truly worthwhile and what is secondary in life.

Ask: In what ways has the church, through the ages, taken the notions of power that Jesus turned upside down and turned them back again? Have you ever experienced the personal power in humility?

Jesus' Last Supper has several meanings for Christians. One is *Eucharist* (from a Greek word meaning "thanksgiving"), which reminds us to take, eat, and be thankful. Another word is *sacrament*, which means a channel or means of grace. A third word comes from the Roman Catholic Church, *Mass*. It means "to be sent" (from the Lord's table into the world). A fourth word is *communion*, which emphasizes fellowship with Jesus Christ. Paul emphasized the fifth word, *memorial*: "Do this in remembrance of me" (1 Corinthians 11:24). Ask group members if we must choose only one meaning, or can we accept them all? Is any meaning more compelling for you? In what way? Does the event of Holy Communion lose some of its power or import if any of those five emphases is missing? If so, how?

Father, into your hands I commit my spirit (23:46a).

13

JESUS EXPERIENCES CALVARY AND RESURRECTION

Luke 23:26–24:53

DIMENSION ONE: WHAT DOES THE BIBLE SAY?

Answer these questions by reading Luke 23:26-56

1. Who carries Jesus' cross behind him? (23:26)

   Simon of Cyrene carries Jesus' cross.

2. What do the women who are in the large number of people who follow Jesus do? (23:27)

   They mourn and wail for Jesus.

3. What does Jesus say to them? (23:28)

   Jesus says, "Do not weep for me; weep for yourselves and for your children."

4. Why does Jesus say this? (23:29)

   They are to weep because a day will come when barren women who have never borne or nursed children will be considered more blessed than those who have.

5. How many other persons are led away with Jesus to be put to death? (23:32)

   They lead away two others, who are criminals, with Jesus to be put to death.

6. Where do they take the three men? (23:33)

   They take the three men "to the place called the Skull."

7. After they crucify the three men, what does Jesus say? (23:34a)

    Jesus says, "Father, forgive them, for they do not know what they are doing."

8. Following Jesus' prayer, what do they do? (23:34b)

    They cast lots to divide up his clothes.

9. Who sneers at, mocks, and insults Jesus and what does each say? (23:35-39)

    1. The rulers sneer, saying, "He saved others; let him save himself if he is God's Messiah, the Chosen One."

    2. The soldiers mock him, saying, "If you are the king of the Jews, save yourself."

    3. One of the criminals insults him, saying, "Aren't you the Messiah? Save yourself and us!"

10. Who defends Jesus? (23:40-41)

    The other criminal, hanging on his cross, says, "Don't you fear God, . . . since you are under the same sentence? We are punished justly, for we are getting what our deeds deserve. But this man has done nothing wrong."

11. What is Jesus' response to the man's request to remember him "when you come into your kingdom"? (23:42-43)

    "Truly I tell you, today you will be with me in paradise."

12. Between noon and three in the afternoon, what two major events take place? (23:44-45)

    Darkness comes over the land for three hours, and the curtain in the temple is torn in two.

13. What are Jesus' last words on the cross? (23:46)

    Jesus' last words are, "Father, into your hands I commit my spirit."

14. When the centurion sees what has taken place, he praises God. What does the centurion say about this event? (23:47)

    The centurion says, "Surely this was a righteous man."

15. What do the various people do at Jesus' death? (23:48-49)

    The spectators return home, beating their breasts (that is, repentant). His acquaintances and the women who followed him from Galilee stand at a distance, watching.

16. Who asks Pilate for Jesus' body? (23:50-52)

    Joseph of Arimathea, "a member of the Council," asks Pilate for Jesus' body.

17. What do the women who have come with Jesus from Galilee do that afternoon? (23:54-56)

    Sabbath is about to begin, so they follow Joseph to see the tomb and how Jesus' body has been laid there; then they return home to prepare spices and perfumes to anoint Jesus' body for burial. Then they observe the Sabbath.

Answer these questions by reading Luke 24

18. What do the women discover when they reach the tomb? (24:2-3)

    They discover the stone rolled away from the tomb; but when they go in, they do not find the body.

19. What are the women wondering about, and who appears to them? (24:4-5)

    They are wondering why the tomb is empty when two men in gleaming clothes stand by them. The men ask why they are looking "for the living among the dead."

20. What do the two men ask the women to remember? (24:6-7)

    The men ask the women to remember what Jesus told them: "The Son of Man must be delivered over to the hands of sinners, be crucified and on the third day be raised again."

21. As two disciples walk toward Emmaus, who joins them? (24:13-15)

    Jesus comes up and walks with them.

22. After Cleopas and his companion summarize what has taken place in Jerusalem during the past three days, what does Jesus say? (24:25-26)

    Jesus chides them for their foolishness and slowness of heart to believe what the prophets have spoken. "Did not the Messiah have to suffer these things and then enter his glory?"

23. What opens the eyes of Cleopas and his companion to Jesus' identity? (24:30-31)
    Jesus becomes known as he breaks the bread and gives thanks.

24. What happens when Cleopas and his companion tell the Eleven and those who are with them about their experience? (24:36)
    Jesus himself stands among them with a word of peace.

DIMENSION TWO: WHAT DOES THE BIBLE MEAN?

The Scripture for this lesson is divided into four themes:
1. From the Cross to the Burial (23:26-56)
2. Discovery of the Empty Tomb (24:1-12)
3. Jesus' Appearances After Resurrection (24:13-43)
4. Christ's Parting From His Disciples (24:44-53)

Luke 23:26-56. As the soldiers lead Jesus and the two criminals away to be crucified, they realize that Jesus cannot carry his cross after all the abuse he has experienced. The whole cross is not put on the back of the criminal, only the crossbeam. The crossbeam will be nailed to a pole, which will then be dropped into a hole. The soldiers seize Simon of Cyrene to carry Jesus' crossbeam.

Mark 15:21 tells us that Simon is the father of Rufus and Alexander. Ancient tradition claims that his two sons became outstanding church leaders. We wonder if they were present with their father that day, preparing to celebrate the Passover. If so, what did they think of the demand placed on their father to carry the heavy crossbeam? Would they experience rejection because their father carried a criminal's crossbeam? Did they see something in their father's face when he returned? What happens to a person who, at first unwillingly, carries a cross in behalf of the Lord? What did Jesus say to Simon, or what did his eyes speak?

Simon was in Jerusalem to celebrate God's passing over Israel and thus bringing them freedom. Jesus also came to set people free. Simon would have heard the voices of the people and especially of the "women who mourned and wailed for [Jesus]." What did Simon think when he heard Jesus say, "Do not weep for me; weep for yourselves and for your children"? If they wept for a guiltless man, such as Jesus, how much more should they weep for the guilty persons who ruthlessly plotted and secured his death? Remember that Jesus also stopped and wept over the beautiful Jerusalem that knew not the thoughts, actions, and emotions that make for peace.

In AD 68, Titus (of Rome) would lead scores of military battalions to destroy Jerusalem and Judah. Women who were barren would thank God that they would not have to watch hunger, cruelty, and death befall their offspring. They would pray for death, that the mountains would fall on them and the hills cover them. (See 23:29-31.)

Luke 23:31 is a proverb: "For if people do these things when the tree is green, what will happen when it is dry?" If the innocent Jesus must suffer so greatly, what will be the fate of the guilty city?

The authorities lead the three men to the place of "the Skull." Whether it has that name because it looks like a skull or because the skulls of crucified persons are lying there, we do not know. Mark (15:22) and Matthew (27:33) call the place Golgotha, which is Aramaic for "The Place of the Skull." The Latin word for skull is *calvary*. The exact location of the Skull is not certain. We do know from Hebrews 13:12 that the place was outside the city gate.

Jesus is crucified between two criminals at the place called the Skull. Crucifixion was a method of Roman execution; the stoning of a person was the Jewish method. Either way was cruel and provided a spectacle for many. Crucifixion involved tying or nailing the outstretched arms of the victim to the crossbeam while it lay on the ground. Then the crossbeam was nailed or lashed to the upright beam, which was then dropped into the hole dug for it. Sometimes the body was supported by a kind of crude wooden saddle projecting from the pole. The feet were nailed or tied to the pole. The body was naked and exposed to sun, wind, flies, and the abuse of spectators. Death usually came by a combination of lack of air, exhaustion, and exposure. After death, the body was usually left to the dogs and buzzards.

Soon Jesus feels the excruciating pain in his nailed hands and feet as the pole drops into its hole with a thud. Jesus prays in anguish, "Father, forgive them, for they do not know what they are doing." What depth of love is required to outweigh the normal curse of pain. Then the soldiers cast lots for Jesus' garments (23:34).

Each of the four Gospels records the gambling for Jesus' garments—which seems to have been the right of those soldiers who carried out the Crucifixion. The major item of interest was his seamless robe. (See John 19:23-25.) Most robes were made by sewing together two long strips (about four feet wide) made of goat hair. Jesus' robe was one continuous cloth, which folded inward (about two feet), and was sewn together at the top. Two holes were made on the sides for sleeves. The robe acted as a cloak by day and a cover for the night.

The soldiers' gambling for the robe fulfills Psalm 22:18. Jesus spoke the opening words of this psalm from the cross, "My God, my God, why have you forsaken me?" (Psalm 22:1), which Matthew reports (Matthew 27:46).

Several groups verbally abuse Jesus. The rulers scoff at him, "He saved others; let him save himself if he is God's Messiah, the Chosen One." The soldiers and even one of the crucified criminals also mock Jesus in the same way. The other criminal replies to the first, "Don't you fear God? . . . We are punished justly. . . . But this man has done nothing wrong." Turning to Jesus, he says, "Jesus, remember me when you come into your kingdom." Jesus answers, "Today you will be with me in paradise."

Then Jesus, crying with a loud voice, says, "Father, into your hands I commit my spirit." Only Luke reports this statement from Psalm 31:5. Luke tells us the personal things that happen, especially to Mary. He writes about the annunciation to Mary. We now understand the words of Simeon to Mary, "A sword will pierce your own soul too" (2:35). Mary, one of the women at the cross, hears her son's last words before death. They are the words she taught him as a small boy—his first prayer, which every loyal Jewish mother taught her child, "Into your hands I commit my spirit; / deliver me, LORD, my faithful God" (Psalm 31:5). How Mary must have treasured his bedtime prayer! And now he prays it as his last words. Mary feels the sword piercing her soul.

We wish we knew the name of the centurion who witnessed Jesus' last words. Could it be the soldier whose faith amazed Jesus (Luke 7) ? Whoever he was, he knew how to praise God; and he now states, "Surely this was a righteous man."

"When all the people who had gathered to witness this sight saw what took place, they beat their breasts and went away." The noncanonical "Gospel of Peter" says, "Then the Jews and the elders and the priests, perceiving what great evil they had done to themselves, began to lament and to say, 'Woe on our sins, the judgment and the end of Jerusalem is drawn nigh'" (7:25). And Jerusalem did fall and was destroyed in AD 70.

In contrast, scores of people who loved and valued Jesus' actions and words were petrified by his physical and mental pain. "All those who knew him, including the women who had followed him from Galilee, stood at a distance, watching these things" (Luke 23:49).

Ask group members to follow along in their Bibles as you read Luke 23:50-56. What can we learn about the man who buries Jesus? (1) His name is Joseph. (2) He is a Jew. (3) He lives in Arimathea. (4) He is a member of the Sanhedrin. (5) He did not consent to the purpose and deeds of the Council (Sanhedrin). (6) He is looking for the kingdom of God. (7) He goes to Pilate and asks for Jesus' body. (8) He takes the body down from the cross and wraps it in a linen shroud. (9) He lays the body in a rock-hewn tomb. The Sabbath is just beginning.

The women from Galilee who accompanied Jesus and have cared for his needs follow Joseph. They see the tomb and how his body is laid. As the Sabbath (Friday evening) came, "they went home and prepared spices and perfumes" (23:56).

Luke 24:1-12. Mark's Gospel tells us that at the end of the Sabbath, the women bought spices so they could anoint the body (Mark 16:1). The women include Mary, the mother of Jesus; Mary Magdalene; Mary, the mother of James the younger; and Salome, the mother of James and John. John probably accompanied Jesus' mother; since John received responsibility for her at the cross when Jesus thoughtfully said, "Woman, here is your son. . . . Here is your mother" (John 19:26-27).

This group of loyal persons goes to the tomb, taking the spices they have prepared. They find the stone rolled away; and upon entering, they do not find the body. However, two men in gleaming clothing stand by them. Frightened, the women bow low. The men say, "Why do you look for the living among the dead?" This statement is tremendous theologically. Jesus Christ cannot be found entombed, nor can he be entombed in creeds or rituals or traditional anthems. Christ was set free from all tombs and is alive throughout our world.

These Galilean woman are something to behold. They are actually the founders of our theological faith. They are the first to see, hear, and speak the good news: Christ is risen. The two radiant men say, "Remember how he [Jesus] told you, while he was still with you in Galilee: 'The Son of Man must be delivered over to the hands of sinners, be crucified and on the third day be raised again.'" The women remember Jesus' words, and they return from the tomb telling all this to the Eleven and to all the rest.

Though the women witness to the disciples, the disciples doubt their words, which "seemed to them like nonsense." The noncanonical "Gospel of Peter" makes an interesting statement. The soldiers guarding Jesus' tomb report to the centurion and elders that they "saw the heavens opened, and two men descend from thence with great light and approach the tomb." These angels rolled away the tomb and entered it. Together, they then reported to Pilate all they had seen, concluding that Jesus has left the tomb and that "truly he was the Son of God." Pilate answers, "I am clear from the blood of the son of God, but this thing seemed good to you." The centurion and soldiers beg Pilate to command them to silence about all they had witnessed "For," they said, "it is better for us to incur the greatest sin before God, than to fall into the hands of the people of the Jews and be stoned." Pilate then ordered the centurion and the soldiers to say nothing (Peter 11:47-49). This conspiracy of silence is supported in Matthew 28:11-15.

Luke 24:13-43. Each of the Gospels includes some post-resurrection interaction between Jesus and his disciples, but Luke alone tells the story of what happened on the road to Emmaus. Cleopas and his companion are going to a village named Emmaus. The question as to who Cleopas's companion is has been debated by scholars for many centuries. Eusebius, an early church historian, thinks it is Luke. John 19:25 implies it is Cleopas's wife. (John says Clopas, not Cleopas.) It may be that Cleopas is one of those sources (Luke 1:2) on whom Luke relied for this kind of story.

On Sunday morning, soon to be called "The Lord's Day" in honor of Jesus' resurrection, two followers of Christ are on their way from Jerusalem to Emmaus (probably about seven miles north). They are discussing the events of the past few days. While talking and discussing together, Jesus (unrecognized) joins them. He asks why they are so serious and sad. Then they tell their story. You might ask three persons to roleplay this scene. It can be quite effective. The actors are these: Jesus, Cleopas, and Cleopas's companion.

Cleopas responds to the stranger's question by saying, "Are you the only one visiting Jerusalem who does not know the things that have happened there in these days?" Jesus asks, "What things?" And they tell him of the plot of the Sanhedrin and how they condemned Jesus to death by crucifixion. They tell of their broken hopes that Jesus was the Messiah, come to redeem Israel. Furthermore, their hopes are dashed by his death and burial in a tomb. Some Galilean women say they went to the tomb where he was buried by order of Pilate, but his body was not there. The women say they saw two "angels" who stated emphatically that he is risen. Moreover, some of the Galilean men went to the tomb; and, truly, he was not there. Where is our Lord?

Soon Jesus interprets the book of Moses (the Torah) and the prophets, helping Cleopas and his companion understand the relationship of Scripture to himself. He shows how the Christ must suffer (and undoubtedly referred to the suffering servant of Isaiah 53). Though their hearts burn within them, they do not recognize Jesus. You might discuss with group members: In what way are the eyes of Cleopas and his companion blinded? They do not see Jesus until the breaking of bread. Do we fail to see him too?

The point is significant: Cleopas and his companion recognize Jesus by the way Jesus prays. His blessings at mealtime reflect his nearness and at-one-ment with God. The style of a pray-er's prayer may reveal Christ's presence.

Cleopas and his companion return to Jerusalem immediately and share their experiences of being in the presence of the risen Lord. As they share, "Jesus himself stood among them." They know the Lord lives.

Luke 24:50-51. Jesus leads his disciples as far as Bethany, where he loved to spend some of his evenings in various homes. At Bethany he lifts up his hands and blesses them. "While he was blessing them, he left them." This parting is called the Ascension. Jesus is "taken up into heaven" from his friends in the sense of now being set free from the bonds of earth; he is no longer bound by the categories of time and space. The risen Lord is everywhere. Time is irrelevant.

DIMENSION THREE: WHAT DOES THE BIBLE MEAN TO ME?

The group may discuss the following topic or use the material in the participant book.

Luke 23:26-49—Christ on the Cross

One of the criminals on the cross turned to the guiltless Christ and said, "Jesus, remember me when you come into your kingdom." What a strange statement to say to a man suffering the tortures of the damned—hands and feet nailed to a scaffold; ridiculed and scoffed at by the religious leaders of the Holy City; the women of Jerusalem weeping at his pain, while the women of Galilee who had ministered to him for three years were in such agony they could only stand, with transfixed emotions and dulled minds, their hearts broken and their Christlike wills paralyzed.

Yet a kingly power reigned on the cross. And even as Jesus had come to set captives free, so his heavenly Father would set him free and raise him above all earthly powers as the King of kings and Lord of lords. He had a moral, aesthetic, righteous at-one-ment with God never known before. He was God's Chosen One through whom all people might know God. For God was revealed in the life, teachings, daily purposes, and death of Jesus of Nazareth, the Christ of God.

Luke states that while the sun's light failed from noon to three p.m., "the curtain of the temple was torn in two." The Holy of Holies was entered only once a year on the Day of Atonement by the high priest. A curtain separated the Holy Place from the Holy of Holies. The symbolism Luke conveys is that now, in Christ, all persons (not just the high priest) can offer prayer. "Anyone who has seen me has seen the Father" (John 14:9).

Especially at Lent we may ask about the seven last words (or sentences) Jesus uttered from the cross. They are drawn from all four Gospels in the New Testament. John has three that do not appear in the other three Gospels; Matthew and Mark have only one, and that does not appear in Luke or in John. Luke has three that do not appear in any other Gospel. Luke's three last words (or sentences) are found in Luke 23:34-46. They were probably remembered by the women from Galilee and became sources for Luke's Gospel.

Consider all the last words:

> First—"My God, my God, why have you forsaken me?" (Matthew 27:46)
> Second—"Father, forgive them, for they do not know what they are doing" (Luke 23:34)
> Third—"Truly I tell you, today you will be with me in paradise" (Luke 23:43)
> Fourth—"Father, into your hands I commit my spirit" (23:46)
> Fifth—"Woman, here is your son." (John 19:26)
> Sixth—"I am thirsty." (John 19:28)
> Seventh—"It is finished." (John 19:30)

What do they tell you was going through Jesus' mind as he was dying? What can they teach us about living in a Christlike way?

A significant personal, as well as theological, concern is about the type of body we have after death. Paul argues strongly that the body Jesus had after his physical death was a spiritual body. (Read 1 Corinthians 15.) Jesus, and we ourselves, die. What we sow (the body) is perishable; what is raised is a spiritual body and therefore imperishable. The Christian lives in the kingdom of God—sometimes for a lifetime; some live there considerably less time. When a Christian dies and is already in the kingdom of God, her or his death is seen as the end of the physical life but the continuation of the spiritual life. The vision of the full abundant life now moves from hope to fulfillment.

Ask: What do you make of the "resurrection of the body"? Review the other Scriptures you recall about what a final resurrection will be (meeting Christ in the air, not having a physicality or earthly relationships like having a spouse, Jesus' empty tomb). What sort of picture does this portray about what happened to Jesus' body? Will what happens to our bodies after death be the same? Does, or should, that have some impact on considering burial versus cremation? How important is it that we know?

CPSIA information can be obtained
at www.ICGtesting.com
Printed in the USA
LVOW04s1940070218

565705LV00009B/65/P